KNIGHT MEMORIAL LIBRARY
DELETED

The Smart Girl's Guide to

TAROT

D1532054

Also by Emmi Fredericks

Fatal Distraction:
Or How I Conquered My Addiction to
Celebrities and Got a Life

As Mariah Fredericks

The True Meaning of Cleavage

Head Games

FEB 10 2005

The Smart Girl's Guide to

TARoT

Emmi Fredericks

Illustrations by Meredith Green

THOMAS DUNNE BOOKS ♠ NEW YORK
ST. MARTIN'S GRIFFIN

KM FEB 1 0 2005 156. 1324
F 852S

For Carin and Katy

May you find the World at the end of
all your readings.

THOMAS DUNNE BOOKS.
An imprint of St. Martin's Press.

THE SMART GIRL'S GUIDE TO TAROT. Copyright © 2004 by Emmi Fredericks.
All rights reserved. Printed in the United States of America. No part of
this book may be used or reproduced in any manner whatsoever without
written permission except in the case of brief quotations embodied in
critical articles or reviews. For information, address St. Martin's Press,
175 Fifth Avenue, New York, N.Y. 10010.

www.stmartins.com

Illustrations copyright© 2004 by Meredith Green.

Book design by Ellen Cipriano

LIBRARY OF CONGRESS CATALOGING-IN-PUBLICATION DATA

Fredericks, Emmi.
The smart girl's guide to tarot / Emmi Fredericks.
p. cm.
ISBN 0-312-32354-9
EAN 978-0312-32354-7
1. Tarot. I. Title

BF1879.T2.F735 2004
133.3'2424—dc22
2004049433

First Edition: October 2004

10 9 8 7 6 5 4 3 2 1

Contents ★

The Cards: The Minor Arcana

Tarot: Cheaper than Zoloft and Less Fattening than Chocolate

*A*lmost every woman has done it at some point in her life—and it's nothing to be ashamed of.

Usually, it starts with a crisis. You get dumped. Or fired. You discover that your roommate is, in fact, a bitch from hell.

It can also start with a yearning. A poignant desire for . . . sex. The chance to quit your job and devote yourself to your art. Or a bus, to run over your bitch-from-hell roommate.

So, what do you do?

First, you bore your friends to death.

Then, you waste countless hours of therapy.

And, finally, when you've reached the breaking point, and nobody, not even your therapist, is talking to you . . .

You go for a tarot reading.

Now, there's no point in denying it. Or claiming the thought never entered your head. We all know that there comes a time when your daily horoscope just isn't enough and you need more info about what lies ahead.

But haven't you noticed that, as with men, a good tarot reading is hard to find? Maybe you have a friend who does readings. In that case, all you have to do is laugh nervously, and say, "Hey, I know it's dumb, but do you think you could do a reading for me sometime?" And then pray she doesn't spread your business all over town.

Or maybe you get a recommendation from someone. "Oh, my God, this woman is amazing. She predicted my cousin's cat would die . . . and it did!" (For some reason, people always recommend readers who give bad news that comes true. I, personally, never take such recommendations. I can make myself crazy on my own, thank you.)

But if you don't have a friend who reads tarot and you can't get a recommendation, then you are forced to take that riskiest of propositions . . .

Roadside Tarot.

You know what I'm talking about. Those places that hang a tatty, worn, white shingle on the door with the words TAROT READINGS and crude drawings of crystal balls and black cats on it?

Yeah, you know the one I mean. The cramped, dinky space with the dodgy folding chair. The old lady who opens your third eye and gives you a reading that could be true, could be not, and is probably the same reading she's been giving all day.

And all the while, you sit there and wonder. . . .

Does she actually know anything, or is she just bullshitting me completely?

Admit it, haven't you spent entire tarot readings trying to guess if this person actually knows anything about you, or if she's making the whole thing up?

Uh, well, yeah.

Of course you have. So, wasn't that a waste of fifteen bucks?

There's another problem with Roadside Tarot. It's usually done by cranky, bored, old women who don't know anything about your life. About the pressures, the contradictions, the lack of visible help anywhere on the horizon. . . .

It's enough to make you crazy. At the very least, mildly neurotic.

Let's face it, given the state of the world today, if you're not neurotic, you're insane.

Why the World Makes the Modern Woman Crazy— and How Tarot Can Save Her Psyche

I'm going to make a confession here. I am a deeply neurotic person.

And that's one of the things that led me to tarot.

I think neurotics get a bad rap. A little anxiety is a perfectly rational response to a world where expectations are high, but control is minimal. A world in which the list of To Dos for the modern woman is long and intimidating.

Have a fabulous job. Be creative. Make money. Be gorgeous . . . and brilliant . . . and have a great boyfriend. In fact, have several. Then find the one that's really perfect and marry him. Have ideal children. (Oh, and don't forget that fabulous, high-paying job. Someone's got to pay for the BabyGap.)

A world that tells you that something as insignificant as a chipped nail or a split infinitive truly matters cannot complain that you're a teensy bit neurotic. Details do matter. Neurotics know God is in the details. But since you're not God, how can you keep track of it all?

Let's take a quick quiz. . . .

1. Do you secretly believe that a misplaced comma on your resume can mean the difference between getting a job and not?
2. In a room full of women, do you generally rate yourself in the bottom third in terms of looks—not because they're so gorgeous and you're so ugly, but because *you* failed to do one little thing (i.e., stick to your diet, get your roots touched up, not wear the sweater that is so comfortable but makes you look fat, etc.)?
3. After a party, do you wake up at 2:30 in the morning thinking, "Oh, my God, why did I *say* that?"
4. At performance review time, are you always surprised when you get a great review—yet think your raise stinks, considering how incredibly hard you work?

We who are neurotic are devout believers in Chaos Theory. We know, *for a fact*, that a leaf falling in the Amazon jungle has a direct effect on whether or not we get a promotion, that guy from the bar calls, or if we win the lottery. Everything is related! Everything is interconnected!

What you want from tarot is a little hint from the universe. A little peek into which way that leaf in the jungle is falling and what it might mean to you.

And a tarot reading can definitely do that for you. But here's something else it can do: it can tell you when you're obsessing about the wrong thing.

All Stressed Out and Nowhere to Go

We're all out there, working and worrying our butts off, trying to get every little thing right. . . .

But are we doing the right things?

I had a friend. She wanted two things out of life: a man and a writing career. My God, the energy she expended "pursuing" her dreams. The number of hair colors she went through, the diets she went on, the writing classes she took, the number of hours she spent bitching about her job because it didn't utilize her true gifts. . . .

Here are two things she never tried:

1. Asking a guy out.
2. Writing something.

Every time I did a tarot reading for her, it turned out exactly the same. No Prince Charming. No Pulitzer prize.

The cards were very kind. They explained why the Universal Santa was not going to give her what she asked for. And it wasn't because her job took all her time or because she was ten pounds overweight.

It was because she was scared. Because she never put herself out there and risked rejection. Every reading I did for that woman turned up the Star reversed, the card of doubt and pessimism, or the Hanged Man reversed, symbol of obsession with false material matters.

We all have our reasons for why we don't have what we want. But you'd be surprised how often they're the wrong reasons. The cards are very good at cutting through the smoke and mirrors we set up in our psyches and getting straight to the heart of the matter. (Sometimes with a buzz saw.)

Knowledge is Power

Here's another thing tarot can do for you: it can show you what you really want out of a situation.

I know that, for God's sake. Why else would I be doing a tarot reading?

Sure about that?

How often has that exasperated friend asked you, "Okay, what do you want to happen?"

And, feeling like a moron, you've said, "I don't know."

Because you *don't* know. You're not sure. For us, most big questions involve lots of *Ifs* and *Unlesses*.

Sure, I want him back, if *he stops acting like a jerk.*

Yes, I want a promotion, unless *it means I have to work twenty-four hours a day for the same pay and have no life.*

And this is where tarot comes in. I offer no statistics on accuracy, but read correctly, the cards always give a coherent version of the future. If nothing else, your gut reaction to the reading will tell you a lot about what you really want out of this situation—and why. If you see good career prospects, but a lot of stress and a narrow life focus, and you think, "Poop," then maybe that promotion wasn't as essential to your happiness as you thought it was.

Nine times out of ten, I've found a tarot reading can offer one of two things:

1. A clear *and accurate* vision of the future. The questioner asks a question, and the cards answer: Yes, you will, or No, you won't.
2. A clear *and feasible* vision of the future. Sometimes, the cards aren't sure where you're headed, because you're not sure. They pick up your strongest vibes and impulses and

give the probable result of those feelings. If you don't like the future cards, carefully examine the past and present cards. See what you can change about yourself to alter the future.

But here's the thing. Whether it's a weather report from the Amazon rain forest or a good look in the psychic mirror, your chances of getting any of these things from Zelda the Mystic are slim. It's probably not even fair to expect it of her. Zelda's not going to know all the conditional little *If This's, Then That's* of your life. How you did this because he said that, and how that meant you just had to do the third thing.

So, why waste fifteen bucks trying to tell if someone's bullshitting you when you can bullshit yourself for free?

Oh, yeah, sure. My past is the Four of Swords and my future is the Hierophant. What the hell does that tell me?

No question about it. The language of many tarot guides can be irritatingly vague. When an answer sounds uncertain or noncommittal, it makes most of us anxious. ("So, will you call me?" "Maybe." "[Argh!]") We deeply fear bad news, but, secretly, we prefer it to no news at all. "No" sucks, but it's better than "maybe." Nobody likes living with uncertainty. We're desperate for answers. Give us a clue! A hint! Anything!

The reason most of us consult "expert" tarot readers is not that we don't know how to lay out a bunch of cards. We just don't know how to interpret them. It's not a matter of checking the definition of individual cards in that little pamphlet that comes with the deck. A reading tells a story. In the same way that you wouldn't just skip to the end of the book to find out who the heroine ends up with, you can't skip to the end of a reading, read the final card, and think you've got an answer to your question.

You have to read the whole story.

I've been doing tarot since my late teens. At first, like most people, I jumped ahead to that final card—Was it the Sun? Was it Death?—and rejoiced, or despaired, accordingly.

But after a while, I began to see that the cards can tell you a frightening amount about your situation. Like any good therapist, they dig way back into the past to find out the root of your current problem, and draw your attention to some of the mistakes and assumptions that could be causing you aggravation.

How do they do this? I have absolutely no clue. (And they're not always right—but who is?) However, over the years, I've come to have a healthy respect for their powers of divination. A reading can give you a glimpse into the future, but it also illuminates the choices you made—and may make—that take you to that point.

What I have tried to do in this book is describe the cards exactly as I would if I were giving you a reading. Of course, I don't know what your question is, but my hope is that by stretching beyond the basic "New Hope/Optimism" definition, I'll teach you to think about the cards in a different way. Once you start reading them as a story with a beginning, middle, and (open) end, they'll stop feeling like a bunch of fortune cookie answers. You'll start making connections and finding meaning you didn't see when you were just jumping to that Final Outcome card.

Wait a minute. You said the cards aren't always right. What did you mean by that? Wrong predictions about the future I can get by myself. I don't even have to be sober.

True. There are times when the cards are not as forthcoming as we'd like. Or as accurate. But, often, the problem is with the interpreter, not the cards.

In my experience, the readings that came out "wrong" came out that way because the news was not something I thought the reader wanted to hear, and so I fudged it.

For example, at one office picnic, a nice woman asked me if I would do a reading because she wanted to know if she was going to get married soon. Not because she had anyone in mind, but because it was important to her to be married.

Ha, I thought. *A modern woman who still feels that she is worth nothing if she is not married. The cards and I will set her straight.*

Now, the cards were not encouraging about her immediate prospects. They pointed out her high level of anxiety over the issue, revealed some family pressure, and produced no Prince of Wands on the horizon.

However . . .

There was some indication that someone would come along in the far distant future, and she would probably get married.

So what did I do? I made it conditional. I said the cards were telling her that she needed to be more independent, more self-defined, not worry so much about getting married, because that was a sure way to put off any decent candidate, and then, maybe, just maybe, her wish might come true.

Five years later, she got married. And from what I can tell, she's even pretty happy.

Now, I didn't do anything terribly wrong. But I hid the fact that the cards had given her an answer to her question—partly because I didn't trust the cards ("My God, what if I tell her she will get married, and she ends up not married, and she hates me?"), and partly because I, personally, didn't think that marriage by itself was a good goal for her to have.

And the point is: *Who cares what I think?*

This woman wasn't asking me to be her therapist; she was asking me to tell her which way that leaf in the Amazon was swinging.

And that's why you need this book. So you can decide what the cards are telling you free and clear of the judgments and biases of other people. Of course, you still have to deal with your own powers of denial and wishful thinking. But I find the cards don't let you get away with much.

Tarot cards are like a good friend. They'll point out when you're being a big, fat moron and cheer you up at the same time. After any tarot reading, you'll see the situation more clearly than you did before—if only because you're coming up against a completely unbiased view of it. How can it be unbiased when you're the one reading it? You, with all your neuroses and hopes and fears and dreams? Believe me: When you're looking at the 10 of Swords, it's hard to be in denial. The cards have a way of getting their message across.

Oh, and there's one more thing . . . .

They're really, really fun.

How Do the Cards Work?

I'll be completely up-front here and say I have no freaking clue. The most rational explanation I've ever read claimed that the cards pick up your emotional and intellectual vibrations as you shuffle them, and give you a portrait of your state of mind, the choices you've been making (whether you know it or not), are likely to make in the future, and what you will face as a result. That's why you have to be really focused when you shuffle them—but more on that later.

It sounds kooky, of course. And yet, how many times have you met someone and thought, *I'm getting a bad vibe off this person.* And how often is your first impression correct? Pretty often, right? There are a million little signals we send out without having the least clue we're doing it. Can cards receive and process such signals? Seems weird to think so. And yet, I have to believe they do, because I've done too many readings that proved uncannily correct.

Now, yes, there are the times when you find out that person who gave you bad vibes was having an off day, and they're actually a fabulous person. And there are times when you're completely muddled and unclear, and the cards are going to reflect that. Personally, I don't believe they work like a Magic 8-Ball, spewing out absolute "Yes You

Will/No You Won't" visions of the future. They're far more interesting and valuable (and accurate) than that. They take a scan of everything that's going on in your brain, heart, spirit, and big toe, and say, "This is where you're headed, sister."

One thing that's interesting: Anytime I've ever done two readings for one question, the cards have punished me for it. They get pissed off and, invariably, they give me a reading that indicates someone who's *way* too involved with the material side of life, a person who needs to take a big step back.

In other words: *Stop pestering us for answers we already gave you!*

Now, some of you might say, "Forget it. Give me the Magic 8-Ball, I want a clear yes or no." But any reading of the future that doesn't make *you* the essential factor is worthless. You're the blueprint; if the cards, or the ball, or the Gypsy fortune-teller don't read you, they're throwing away all the most important data.

No one controls everything in her life.

But no one has more control over your life than you.

So, go forth, and seek the answers to your questions.

How to Do a Reading

The Question

A *good reading starts with a good question. Many people begin with* questions that are vague, or open ended, such as "Will I be happy?" or "What's my life going to be like?" Questions like these can't possibly be answered by ten cards—or by anyone else but you, for that matter.

Try to make your question as specific as possible. Choose one area of your life: love, career, family matters—as opposed to . . . everything. Focus on something you hope for in a time period ranging from the next few weeks to the next two years. The best readings come from issues that are pressing *now*, situations that feel immediate and relevant to your life.

Try not to ask questions about other people's lives. For example: "My sister's getting married. Will she be happy?" You're the one shuffling the cards. They're picking up your vibes, your emotions, your hopes, dreams, etc. The cards can tell you how your sister's wedding affects you or what your own prospects for marriage might be. But they don't know from your sister, unless she's sitting at the table, in which case, hand the deck over to her.

Don't ask a question about something you don't care about. Frankly, the best questions come from the stuff that's driving you crazy, the thoughts and emotions that are bouncing around in your brain, clamoring, screeching, whining, until you just want to yell, "SHUT UP!"

That exact point can be a very good time to do a reading. Your emotions are intense, your nerves are raw, everything's exposed (hope you've got the curtains drawn). The cards have a lot to work with.

Here are a few examples of Bad Question versus Good Question. . . .

Bad Question: What should I do with my life?
Good Question: I've been offered a well-paying but boring job. Should I take it?

Bad Question: Will I fall in love?
Good Question: I really like this guy. Do I have a shot?
Good Question: I'd like to start dating this year. Will I?
Good Question: I can't seem to get laid. Why?

Bad Question: Will I be happy?
Good Question: I'm feeling really lousy right now. Can I hope that things will turn around?

Good questions often revolve around choices. Choices between jobs, career paths, lovers. "Should I quit my job?" "Should I dump him?" "Should I go back to grad school?" Better yet, "If I quit, will I be happy in my new job?" "If I dump him, will I regret it?" "If I go back to grad school, will I be destitute?"

Specific, significant, and timely—these are the three elements of a good tarot question.

Doing the Tarot Shuffle

The next important element of a good tarot reading is the shuffle. Once you have your question in mind, pick up the deck and start shuffling it. Focus on your question as you shuffle. Open up the subconscious and let all those demons out. "I hate him," "I feel like shit," "I want to be famous"—all that juvenile crap. Try to recall key moments of the story so far: images, words, feelings. It doesn't have to be coherent thought. Just pour all your emotion and perception surrounding this issue into the cards.

When are you done shuffling? When you feel done. If you insist on having a range, I'll tell you that most people seem to go for four to seven shuffles. But it's all about when you feel like you've communicated as much of your issue to the cards as you can.

Remember, the last reading is still in the cards. The cards that turned up in that reading may have just been placed on top of the deck afterwards. You want to shuffle enough so that you don't get the remnants of someone else's business mixed up in yours.

Put Your Cards on the Table

There are lots of different tarot spreads. Some involve three or four cards, some involve practically the whole deck. I like the ten-card spread. It's concentrated, yet comprehensive. It looks like this. . . .

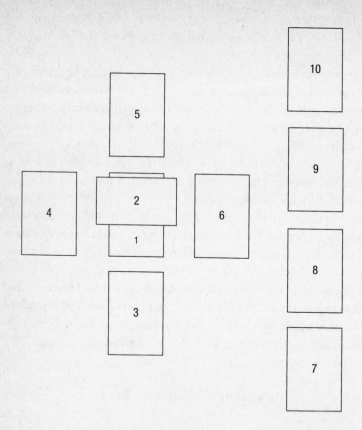

So, lay your cards out in the right order and in the right positions. And now that we've got our cards nicely laid out on the table, it's time to ask: What do these positions mean?

Card Number One (Present Position)
As befits its position in the center of the spread, the first card is the core of the situation as it exists *right now*. It's your state of mind, the environment you're dealing with, the emotional set up of the whole kit-and-caboodle. This card should echo your question in some way.

Card Number Two (Immediate Influence)
This card reflects a counter, or outside, influence. It can act in direct opposition to the first card, but sometimes the relationship is more

complex. Often, when we do a reading, we're feeling torn or blocked in some way. The two cards together can represent the forces that got us into that situation. For example, a strong desire to be creative crossed by a desperate need for cash. Or a yearning for love crossed by crippling insecurity. Or a determination to gain career advancement crossed by the big fat asshole who is your boss. Try to see how the two cards interact. This card is always read as being in the upright position, never reversed.

Card Number Three (Distant Past)

I call this the "Freudian" card. It represents the foundation of the issue, something that happened long ago that's having a big impact on your present situation. Mommy and daddy fought constantly, now I have huge trust issues. Mommy and daddy never had enough money, so I'm saddled with huge college loans and a sense of financial desperation. If the material impact isn't obvious, what you need to think about is how this person, event, or emotion may be affecting your current assumptions and choices.

Card Number Four (Recent Past)

This card addresses the recent events or influences in the situation. I usually think of the time span as a few weeks to a few months, but with the emphasis on "recent." They're often close enough that this card should be instantly recognizable, the memory of it still fresh.

Now we come to the first of the three future cards. Tarot acknowledges that the future is a complex thing. It's not only what you bring to it, it also involves outside influences. So the ten-card reading examines the future from three different angles.

Card Number Five (Goal)

This is the first of three future cards. It represents the best or the worst that can come out of this situation. It's a sort of distillation of all the emotions and events into their purest possible outcome. If it's a positive card, it suggests how much you can achieve if you try. If negative, it's a warning about the potential for disaster. Neither of these is set in stone. One is something to strive for, the other is something to avoid.

Card Number Six (Future Influence)

This is a power—either within yourself or outside of yourself—that will come into play in the near future. It could be an individual who will help you achieve what you want. It could be a period of stubbornness and self-doubt that will hold you back. Look to see how it might relate to Card Number Two, which is your present influence.

Card Number Seven (The Questioner)

This is you, how you see yourself and your situation. You might say, "Well, I know that, for God's sake!" But it's always helpful to get a second opinion. If, for example, other cards indicate prosperity and well-being, and this card comes up misery and deprivation, you might be in a slightly pessimistic mood. Conversely, if the other cards are all woe and misery, and this one comes up joy and bright expectations, check your denial meter. It's a chance to see what you're bringing to the table.

Card Number Eight (Environment/Outside View)

This is a fascinating card in conjunction with Card Number Seven, because it tells you how other people see you. Out of all the cards, with the possible exception of Number Three, this one may be the most baffling. We seldom see ourselves as others do, and even the most perceptive may have trouble reconciling their vision of themselves with other people's vision of them. Bear in mind, too, there are a lot of people in your life; ergo, opinions may conflict, so you may see some contradictions in this card.

Card Number Nine (Hopes and Fears)

This is always where you want to see the Big Bad News cards. Unlike Card Number Five, Number Nine is a dream. This card is not the future; only what you hope or fear the future holds. This is illuminating in a lot of different ways. If your loyalties are divided, it may show you where your heart really lies. If you're looking for marriage, and a money card turns up, it's a clue about your priorities. If you're looking for employment, and the Devil turns up, that tells you something about your fear of commitment.

Card Number Ten (The Final Outcome)

Sound trumpets, here it is, the FINAL OUTCOME! This is the result of all the efforts, emotions, and influences indicated in the rest of the reading. As such, it is subject to change. If you don't like the Final Outcome, look at the other cards to see what's pushing you down the wrong path.

Some outcomes are more final than others. If the card is a wimpy, maybe-this–maybe-that, Minor Arcana card, it may represent a result that is soon to come, but not necessarily long-lasting. Events may be too chaotic to read right now. You might be too chaotic to read right now.

But if it's a Major Arcana card, or one of the strong Minor Arcana, then the cards are giving you a definite signal of the nature of this situation for some time to come.

May you see the World and steer clear of the Devil in every reading.

Let's Recap

To begin a reading. . .

1. Choose your question.
2. Shuffle the deck.
3. Lay out the cards.

Other Things to Think About

Many books suggest picking what's called a "Significator"—a card that represents you—and placing it in the center. You then lay the first card over it, and continue on in the same way. I tried using Significators for a while, and I have to say they made no discernible difference in the reading. Often, women are told to pick one of the Queens, the one they feel best reflects their personality. (Often you do it based on appearance. "Choose this card for a black-haired woman," "Choose this card for a fair woman," and so on. Frankly, in the age of Clairol, this seems silly, and I've never done it.)

In my experience, no one ever found a queen that really matched her, and the whole exercise was a distraction. But if the idea of a Significator appeals to you, go ahead and pick one.

Why You Shouldn't Skip to the Final Outcome Card

As should be clear by now, the future is comprised of a lot of different elements: your past, your expectations, how people see you . . . all of these factors play a part. Change any one of them and you'd get a different reading.

So don't skip to that final card, hoping to see a Yay! or Boo! Some final outcomes are so clear and strong, it is possible to see Dark Omen or Happy Ending in them, but many are not. And if you don't read the other cards, you'll have no idea how you get there or how to change course.

Reversed Cards

Some books recommend that if more than half the cards in a reading are reversed, you might try reading them as if they were right-side-up. Does that mean you should read the cards that are right-side-up as reversed? I don't know.

I like to take the cards at their word; it's way too tempting to change the meaning of a reversed card, as it can often mean the difference between a happy outcome and an unhappy one. What I do if I get a reading that's heavy on reversed cards is wait a bit, then try it again.

Should I Straighten Out My Deck Every So Often?

The cards get to know you. You've shuffled a lot of emotion and thought into them. But if you're getting the same cards over and over, then you might consider returning the deck to its original pristine condition. I never have, but that doesn't mean you shouldn't.

Any Particular Deck I Should Use?

I used a sort of no-name, beginner's tarot deck for many years and grew quite attached to it. But when the Three of Swords went missing, I had to face the fact that I needed a new deck. When I went shopping, I discovered there are a frightening variety of tarot decks out there, from decks that cater to the goddess crowd, to ones that appeal to the baseball enthusiast.

I went with the classic Rider Tarot Deck, which was created by Arthur Edward Waite. Pamela Colman Smith's illustrations are evocative and specific, giving you an excellent sense of the card's meaning. I would recommend this one—unless you happen to be a goddess or baseball enthusiast.

The illustrations in this book don't exist as a tarot deck yet. We chose Meredith Green's images because we wanted to break away from the standard visions of queens and knights and give tarot a fresh, contemporary look. Her queens and maidens are women any of us can relate to. Hopefully, her deck will soon be available!

Strange but True
Tales of Tarot Number One

The Friend Who Went to Paris

Yeah, it's all crap, but it's still kind of interesting." Isn't that what we all say when we first get into tarot? We don't really *believe* in it, but you know . . . .

Here is the strange but *absolutely true* story of the reading that made me believe.

Very early on in my tarot reading career, I had a friend who went to study art in Paris. There she met . . . yep, you guessed it, a guy. A fabulous, artistic-type guy who was madly in love with her. She had hit the romantic jackpot. She came back to America and announced to her parents that she was quitting school and going to live with the love of her life.

Needless to say, mom and dad were not thrilled. But my friend said, *Tant pis, I'm going anyway.*

So, the week before she left, we decided to do a tarot reading for her future in France. Laying out the cards, I fully expected a reading full of passion, art, and lots and lots of sex.

Instead, this was, without question, the *worst* reading I had ever seen. Death Reversed was in her future. The final outcome card was the Devil. Strife, misery, false hopes, and deception everywhere you looked.

Frantically, we tried to interpret the reading positively. Death, well, that meant a new life. And the Devil, well, maybe that was the lingering effect of her parents' disapproval. It wasn't that we questioned the cards; we just thought we were reading them wrong. Because she was going to go to Paris and live happily ever after, right?

Well, her first clue that maybe the cards were right, and we were wrong, was when she arrived at the apartment of her beloved and found another woman already living there.

Pas de problem, said her beloved. *She's just a friend.*

Needless to say, he was telling his "friend" the exact same thing about my friend. A month passed before the two "friends" decided to compare notes. And that was just the beginning of the ugliness . . . .

Two months later, she returned to America a sadder, wiser woman.

And, ever since then, I have never once said it's all crap.

The Cards

The Major Arcana

*T*here are seventy-eight cards in the tarot deck: twenty-two Major Arcana cards and fifty-six Minor, or Lesser, Arcana cards. The Major Arcana are the cards everyone associates with tarot: The Fool, Death, the Lovers . . . . The Minor Arcana are made up of four suits—cups, swords, pentacles, and wands—that represent different aspects of life.

The Major Arcana are sometimes considered "stronger" cards, more definitive and long-lasting in their predictions. Certainly they're powerful in their symbolism, and so we start with them. Bear in mind, these interpretations are derived from two decades of tarot readings and a variety of sources. I've found one source more accurate on some cards, another source on other cards. As a result, these interpretations will not exactly match any book or booklet you may already have.

THE FOOL

"O noble fool! A worthy fool! Motley's the only wear."

—As You Like It

The traditional definition of the Fool is not a flattering one. The contemporary equivalent might be Wile E. Coyote, chasing the Road Runner and going headlong over the cliff—except that the Fool is much less neurotically goal-oriented than Wile E. Coyote.

Nonetheless, the overall impression is . . . cluelessness. Immaturity. Failure to see life's realities. The Fool just dances along on her merry way, unable to see the very shaky ground she's standing on. Perhaps she doesn't want to. Perhaps that's why she's dancing so fast and so frantically. This card also indicates wild energy and enthusiasm.

So, if this card turns up in a present or future position, or in any of the positions that represent the reader, you must carefully assess your situation. This mindset talks you into marrying someone you've known for six weeks. Or quitting a perfectly decent job because you feel stifled and must be true to your art. Or dropping out of college to see the world. There's a great *yee-haw!* feeling to it, the exhilaration that comes with saying *Screw it! I gotta be me!* Your goal may be reasonable—but are you going about it in a way that will actually achieve that goal . . . or are you just running away? Ask yourself: Is my vision realistic? If you can't be honest with yourself, get someone else to be honest with you.

However, there is something undeniably appealing about the Fool, a subversive freedom that we all feel drawn to at some point in our lives. No wonder manic-depressive Jacques declares, "Motley's the only wear." There's probably a touch of the Fool in every significant step you take in life. Is it possible to strike a balance between carefree and cautious? Probably not. But if you err on the side of caution most of the time, you probably should give yourself permission to try carefree once in a while. Just watch out for that cliff.

THE FOOL REVERSED

In simplest terms, the Fool Reversed can be seen as the "after photo" of the Fool. One stepping boldly forward, the second flat on her face with the banana peel on her head. She represents a mistake. A bad choice. One of those times in life you have to say, I goofed, whether in your choice of lover, job, or in passing along that secret that you swore never, ever to tell a living soul.

But the Fool Reversed reminds us that there are two ways to screw up in life: by making the wrong choice and by making no choice. In most definitions of the Fool Reversed, you find the words "bad decision," but you also find the words "apathy" and "negligence." In contrast to her fearless, feckless counterpart, the Fool Reversed often hangs back, too worried about everything that could go wrong to take that first step forward. Even if she's not particularly thrilled with how her life is going, she's too depressed and apathetic to change it. "What can *I* do?" moans this fatalistic femme. She thinks she's made choices but, really, she's just gone along for the ride, and now she's not happy with where she ended up.

Here it will be up to the reader to admit how much energy she's putting into directing her own life. If she's a take-charge kind of gal who's recently made a big change, this might indicate the change won't turn out the way she wanted. This is a bad card to see, for example, in the future of someone planning to get married.

But if her dreams and her reality don't match up, if she's always finding reasons that she *can't*, then she has to start challenging some of the assumptions that keep her locked in her present unpleasant position. Start breaking some rules. Make the great leap forward. Even if you end up with a banana peel on your head, you'll be better off in the long run.

THE MAGICIAN

"Don't lose confidence in an effect because it has been presented many times before. An old trick in 'good hands' is always new. Just see to it that yours are 'good hands.'"

—Harry Houdini

Is there anything more satisfying than a good magic trick? The pleasure of watching someone in complete control of events, able to make the audience look wherever she wants them to, until she's ready to pull the proverbial rabbit out of a hat?

Conversely, is there anything more annoying than being fooled?

Where to draw the line between performance and deception—that's one of the questions raised by the Magician. Generally, it's a positive image, something you'd like to see in any career-related question. It represents diplomacy, adroitness, self-confidence—a smooth tongue, and a certain flair. The kind of person who can put together a PowerPoint presentation in a day and astound everyone with her cleverness and originality. You'll hear whispers of "That girl's going places," as you walk by.

It also represents the realms of creativity and imagination. Got an audition coming up? You'll wow them. Starting that novel? Poof! No more writer's block.

Oh, but then, there's that nasty word—deception. It doesn't turn up in every definition of this card, but often enough to note. I take it as a warning to this golden girl: don't mistake veneer for value. Sure, there'll be days when you just don't have it and you have to tap dance your way through. But you can only fool some of the people some of the time and so on. If your passion for your work is gone, you won't be able to fake it for long. Much better to try something or somewhere new. Wake up that excitement and energy that got everyone talking about you in the first place.

THE MAGICIAN REVERSED

Here we see the opposite aspects of the clever, deft sorceress in the Magician. Turn her upside down and several things can happen. The first is that she gets butterfingers. So clumsy and inept, this girl can't shuffle a deck of cards without spraying them all over the place. The second is she becomes uneasy, nervous—possibly even a little depressed. All that imagination and creativity turns into neurosis and insecurity.

The third—and most disquieting of all—is she retains her powers, but she uses them for ill rather than for good. We all know people like this, cute little charmers who can wrap anyone around their finger (or any other part of their anatomy). There's something predatory about this creature; she doesn't claw her way up the ladder or purloin someone's guy because she loves her job or that gent—it's all about the conquest. She has to be able to make people see what she wants them to see and reinforce that winning image of herself again and again, usually at someone else's expense.

We talked about the nature of deception in the Magician. When the Magician is reversed, the darker nature of deception—falseness, lying, cheating—comes to the forefront. This isn't razzle-dazzle, this is a nasty, shabby trick.

So if the Magician Reversed turns up in your present or future, you need to think about what feats you're trying to pull off and whether you really feel confident enough to do it with style. Maybe you need some more preparation. You may end up disappointed, otherwise. If, however, the word "deception" rang big bells in your head, start thinking about what areas in your life feel . . . unreal. Are you faking it? If so, where? Pull that rabbit out of the hat and take a good, long look at it.

THE HIGH PRIESTESS

"We keep thinking of deity as a kind of fact somewhere; God as fact. God is simply our own notion of something that is symbolic of transcendence and mystery. The mystery is what's important."

—JOSEPH CAMPBELL.

One of the most inscrutable cards in the entire tarot deck, the High Priestess may make you think of your old math teacher—the one you hated because she was so tough on you, but whom you secretly wanted to please. There's something a little forbidding about the High Priestess; she's all about secrets. But, accordingly, she's also about trust, discretion, maturity, and the power that comes with them. She doesn't need anyone's approval, and she doesn't blab anyone's personal business. Neither should you, if she comes up in the future. Warning: Stay far away from the madding crowd. Don't have that third drink with the office pals. It'll only lead to trouble. Is she a person? An influence? An approach to life? Well, she's any of the above. Sure, she could be your boss or your mother: some powerful female swooping down to wreak havoc in your well-disordered life with her gentle hints that you could be doing better for yourself. But she could also be you. Yes, she could. Even if you've never had a substance-free serene moment in your adult life, there's always a first time.

Now, if you're asking about love, this is not necessarily a card you want to see. The High Priestess is wise, perceptive, and serene. The words platonic and celibate could also apply. For some, that could be unwelcome news. But for others, it could be a welcome change of pace, particularly if you've been feeling buffeted on the shores of love.

Finally, the High Priestess represents secrets, the unrevealed future. The reader may find this wildly frustrating, as the whole point of a tarot reading is to find out what will happen! But you may have to accept that not all the pieces are in place at this point in time. There's a key element of this situation that has yet to make itself known. In the meantime, you'll just have to wait and see.

THE HIGH PRIESTESS REVERSED

Ever know a couple who got married a few months after they met? Their passion was just so strong, their connection so instant and intense—they just *had* to let love have its day? Then, a few months later, they realized they didn't know the first thing about each other—and what they had found out didn't thrill them. The sex was dead, and they were wondering, *What the hell was I thinking?*

If you'd done a reading for these two lovers before they got married, the High Priestess Reversed would have warned them.

We tend to associate passion with good things: commitment, drama, nooky. Reticence, self-restraint . . . feh. Those things can sound painfully anal to us. But, in both her positions, the High Priestess reminds us of the value of being a grown-up. If she turns up reversed in the future, know that you're going to be thinking with your loins, not your brains. Your judgment is going to be superficial and probably flawed. Don't make any big leaps right now. You will almost certainly regret it.

There are other kinds of passion, as well. Political passion, righteousness, that kind thing. You may feel strongly that you know what the right thing is and it's up to *you* to do it. Proceed with some caution. You may not have all the facts or you may be unaware of the repercussions "the right thing" could lead to.

The High Priestess right side up is fully aware that life is a complex business. It's very difficult to "know" anything for certain. Wisdom takes time and effort to accrue. If she turns upside down in your reading, you know: Now is not the time to listen to your heart. It's cheatin' you.

THE EMPRESS

"I thank God that I am endued with such qualities that if I were turned out of the Realm in my petticoat I were able to live in any place in Christendom."

—ELIZABETH I

When discussing the Empress, you come up against an arcane notion of the center of a woman's power, i.e., her womb. "Fruitful" is the key word associated with the Empress, along with "fertility, motherhood, fecundity . . ." you get the picture.

That's great news for anyone looking to start a family, but it might be somewhat disappointing to those who prefer to see themselves in conquering mode, saber drawn, ready to strike.

However, let's examine the Empress further. She embodies all things female. Mom, sister, best friend . . . . But she also represents what the PR reps for Elizabeth I and Victoria might have tried to convey: stability. Power used, not in the aggressive sense, but in a nurturing, supportive sense. A strong, wealthy ruler reigning over a peaceful kingdom where all are well-fed. Science and the arts flourish. Disease is eradicated, and so on.

So, for those of you with CEO-size dreams, this card will make you happy. Start thinking about ruling with strength and benevolence, dousing petty squabbles, motivating people to do their best, creating a happy work environment. And let's not forget that fruitfulness and creativity are strongly linked, so this card is good news for artists and writers, as well. This is a card of action and initiative.

Some look at the Empress and see a certain secretive quality. Clandestine dealings, the unknown. This could be related to the Victorian obsession with women as mysterious, unknowable creatures— or it could reflect a painful fact of leadership. Remember the elaborate wigs and egg white face of Elizabeth I. Appearances must be maintained. You must seem strong, even when you don't feel strong. Any mother will know exactly what this means.

THE EMPRESS REVERSED

The meaning of the Empress Reversed depends to some degree on how you might choose to read the Empress Right Side Up; either as a vibrant symbol of fecundity and creativity, or as a secretive, reserved type.

I confess I lean toward the Empress as Life Force. So, if I see her upside down, I see all delay, self-doubt, procrastination. A big fat ditherer, the Empress Reversed occupies herself with a million small details so she can't focus on what she really needs and wants to do. If she turns up in your future, you should be wary of any impulse or excuse that keeps you from pursuing your goals.

I should also note here that if the questioner is asking about starting a family, this is obviously not a good card to see in a future position. It could also indicate some tumult in family life: all that stable, cooperative energy going haywire.

Second, let's deal with the aspect of the Empress that's about secrecy and pretense. In this interpretation, the Empress Reversed is a good thing. She's great at blurting out thoughts and feelings that you—or someone close to you—has kept hidden for way too long. Sure, telling or hearing the truth can hurt, but isn't everything clearer afterwards? If the questioner is embroiled in a difficult situation and they can't pinpoint the exact source of the problem ("I just feel he's not honest with me." "I don't know why I don't care anymore."), this card might be exactly what they're looking for. Specifically, it predicts a time when things that have grown tangled and complicated unravel, freeing everyone up, and letting them move on.

THE EMPEROR

"The world begged me to govern it."

—NAPOLEON

Napoleon, Caesar, Bill Gates . . . the primary quality associated with His Imperial Majesty is Pow-ah. Power in the most idealized male sense: authority, wealth, protection. The triumph of reason and intellect over sentiment and emotion.

Oh, and war. Whereas the Empress maintains her empire through her people skills, the Emperor inclines more to simply mowing down any unruly savages who fail to see the benefits of his rule.

But we shouldn't let a jaundiced view of the military affect the way we see the Emperor. A positive figure, he symbolizes strength, order, and calm. Someone's got to be in charge, for God's sake. He's not the bash-and-grab type. He uses his power for the benefit of all.

So, who is he? Well, consider the obvious possibilities: dad, brother, husband. You could also add, boss. You could also add, large corporation. If you're in a job hunting mode, this card in the future might indicate that you'll find a place at a big fat conglomerate with great benefits. Conversely, if you see it in the past, it could mean you have an Electra Complex. Does your heart belong to Daddy? How does your boyfriend feel about that?

What should you think when you see the Emperor? Consider any strong male influences in your life; check to make sure that the other cards don't indicate that his sway over you has, or will, become too great or malign in some way. Do you need a savior right now, someone to sweep in and save the day? The Emperor may represent someone who will do so.

But if he doesn't ring any bells in terms of people you know, you might look inward and find these imperial qualities in yourself. Are you feeling the itch to dominate? Do you hear a little voice telling you you could run things so much better? That everyone's lives would be easier if you were in charge? Maybe you should give in to your imperial tendencies. This card certainly indicates you have the power to do so.

THE EMPEROR REVERSED

The Emperor depicts the razor's edge between authority and autocracy. The Emperor Reversed shows you the thin line between niceness and wimpishness. The two not-so-contradictory definitions of the Emperor Reversed are compassion and weakness.

On the one hand, we have an emphasis on benevolence. Kindness to those weaker than ourselves. The ability to give credit to those who deserve it—all traits we like to see in ourselves and in those who have some power in our lives.

However, the Emperor Reversed can be a big fat wimp. Indecisive and ineffective, when faced with a tough decision, he'll put it off until it's become a much bigger mess than it had to be. Maybe he's worried about hurting people's feelings, maybe he doesn't want to be the bad guy. But, the fact is, someone has to be.

When a card with this kind of split turns up, it's a call to examine the dynamic in your life that represents the dichotomy. The Emperor Reversed could be you, it could be the person you're dealing with, or it could be both. Overall, it could represent a situation that's stalled out because no one wants to be the villain and call it like it is. No one wants to say the relationship is over. No one wants to call a member of the team lazy or unskilled. No one wants to say your sister should just get over her ex-husband already and move on.

If the other cards in your reading indicate bullying and abuse, this card may feel like a bright spot; finally, someone who uses their power for good instead of evil! If it comes up in a reading about a big issue in your life, something where you need to take charge, it may signal a dangerous bout of indecisiveness on your part. This card strongly indicates that you need to look at all the other cards and be as honest with yourself as possible.

THE HIEROPHANT

"If I repent of anything, it is very likely to be my good behavior."

—HENRY DAVID THOREAU

"What the hell is a hierophant?" is usually what you hear when this card shows up. For your general information, a hierophant is a priest of ancient Greece, the keeper of the Eleusinian mysteries. Interesting, but not very revealing about your situation.

Almost every woman should pay attention to the Hierophant because it represents the crossroads between goodness and passivity. One the one hand, the Hierophant conjures images of kindness, forgiveness, and compassion. On the other hand, it's a vision of conformity, fear, outdated ideas, and desperate need for approval. He is both the better side of organized religion in his focus on charity and humanity, and the less great side in his adherence to rules and negation of individuality.

So, how to reconcile all this and decide what this card means for you? Well, let's start with a simple question. Do you, by any chance, have a martyr complex? Does everyone turn to you in a crisis? Do you give and give and give? Do you have a charming and irresponsible lover who demands you take care of him? Are you the greatest gal in the office, the one who does all the shitwork and never complains?

Do you sometimes want to scream, "Do it yourself!" Do you

sometimes feel filled with rage at those who work less hard than yourself? Do you sometimes wonder if you're too critical and judgmental?

If you see this card in your reading, you should be aware that sometimes we do the right thing because we want to, and sometimes because we're afraid not to. Has your need to be liked put a big Kick Me sign on your back? Is the primary pleasure you derive from giving to others a chance to feel superior to them?

Possibly not. The Hierophant doesn't have to represent fear and conformity; it can mean genuine kindness and compassion. It may mean you are giving a lot right now, it may represent someone from whom you seek help. But its contradictions remind us of the importance of sincerity and self-awareness. Sometimes you have to do the right thing for the wrong reasons. The world is too complicated for all sincerity all the time. But you must know when to say when.

THE HIEROPHANT REVERSED

The Hierophant is a complicated card in both its incarnations. The definitions for each have their positive and negative points. But, in general, the Hierophant right side up makes a stronger case for mercy and caring and true connection, the Hierophant Reversed makes a stronger case for patsy.

If you see this card upside down in the present or future in your reading, there's a strong chance that you're loving unwisely and not well. This card means weakness, credulity, vulnerability—generosity to the wrong person and probably for the wrong reasons.

See the Hierophant Reversed in the past and it may represent a past relationship you currently mourn. Get out of the black clothes. It wasn't worth it. You gave and got very little in return. You're better off without him or her.

Or, maybe, you're working flat out at the office for a demanding boss, giving up time that should be used for yourself. If so, then ask: Why am I putting in all this extra effort? Do I expect a raise or promotion? Will I really get that raise or promotion? If not, don't persuade yourself that the work is not "extra." Either find a reason to do it or stop doing it.

Are you in a relationship and wondering if you're putting a lot more into it than your partner? Bad news, you are. More bad news, they may not be worth it. You may be getting all they have to give. Again, ask yourself, is it enough?

The good news is, you have control. Someone may be taking you for a ride, but it's most likely yourself. The other party may wish you'd calm down, stop doing quite so much. Try pulling back; the results will amaze you.

THE LOVERS

Frankie and Johnny were lovers,
my gawd, how they could love.
Swore to be true to each other,
true as the stars above . . .

—TRADITIONAL BALLAD

So many famous lovers in history: Antony and Cleopatra, Tristan and Isolde, Bill and Monica . . . .

And, yet, who do we find depicted in the Lovers? Adam and Eve. That's right—and *before* the Fall. The World's First Couple, when they lived blissful and innocent in their Garden of Eden (although that Serpent lurks behind Eve, and you can bet he's already whispering in her ear).

The Lovers is, of course, *the* card anyone wants to see at the end of a reading about love. All those questions—Will he call? Will I get sex soon? Is my relationship okay?—can find a happy ending in the

Lovers. But this card shows us a particular kind of happiness, with its own pluses and minuses.

The Lovers are happy, happy, happy . . . but they're a little clueless. This card depicts a relationship in its earliest, idealistic stages. It has yet to be tested by serpents, annoying friends, different movie tastes, and those charming flaws and insecurities we all have. It's a wonderful time in a relationship—the dizzy, fizzy time when you are so *in lerve*. It's a rarity, and you should cherish it.

But it's not yet a fully formed, tested partnership.

Now, some of you will say, Great! I don't want mature, reasonable, blah, blah, blah. I want fireworks and romance and infatuation. I want fantastic, wild sex. Well, with this card, you've got it. But sexual rapture time is one of the most "innocent" stages of a relationship. Either you solve most of your problems in bed, or else you're so happy to be having sex that you're willing to overlook a lot of things. Either way, you're dealing with each other on a primal, not terribly complex level.

(Didn't ask about a love relationship? Then the Lovers represents a state of idyllic happiness with *something* new in your life. A new home, new boss, new diet. You're so deliriously happy, you have the energy of ten. And whatever it is looks to be a good match for you— just keep that thought when you come back down to earth.)

You can also think of the Lovers as the *rebirth* of passion and idealism in a relationship. If you've been with someone a while, and you're feeling kind of stale and taken for granted, this card in a future position indicates that the romance can come back—you just have to junk some of the emotional crap that's built up over years of being together: the resentments, the disappointments, the hurts. One year, ten years, no matter how long, you can return to the State of Ga-Ga. And this time, you already know he's not the greatest with remembering birthdays and he hates romantic comedies, so there's no ugly shock.

THE LOVERS REVERSED

. . . he was her man,
but he done her wrong.

It's the fight he picks with your friends. It's the party where he spends more time talking to his ex than to you. It's the yawn right in the middle of your description of your day.

It's the failed test.

Some—many—tests in a relationship are bullshit. No one should have to get a passing grade to be loved. So don't think of the Lovers Reversed as a failed test. Think of it as that first moment when you think, "Maybe he's not Mr. Wonderful." And, sadly, you're probably right.

If you see the Lovers Reversed anywhere in your reading, it's a strong sign that your current relationship is not grounded in reality. If you see it in the past, it might indicate you had overly starry visions when you began; maybe you've grown out of those. If it turns up in the future, you might be about to stub your toe on his feet of clay. Have you reached the breaking point? Look to the other cards to see the overall picture.

Or, maybe, you don't have a partner yet. Maybe you want one and can't figure out why he or she has not materialized. If so, start thinking about your expectations and your approach. Astonishingly, many of us have the goofiest ideas about what an intimate connection means. Often we hunt aspirationally: I'm not gorgeous, hip, and fabulous, but I want a gorgeous, hip, fabulous man because that will mean I am, too. The fact that such a person will probably bore you because they're too busy being fabulous seems unimportant at this point.

It never hurts to talk to a friend you can truly trust, someone who seems to get the whole dating and love thing. Be brutally honest with them about your worries and ask for brutal honesty in return. Your eyes should be clear before you let someone else put stars in them.

THE CHARIOT

Little Red Corvette
Baby, you've got to slow down....

—PRINCE

Two things come to mind when you look at the Chariot: Ben and Hur. Charlton Heston racing along at breakneck speed, the crack of the whip, the dangerous swerve of the chariot as it rounds the turn. . . .

This image gives some idea of the mood of the Chariot. It's a strong, positive, heroic image, but it's also a little anxiety-provoking. It raises the question: How much do you have to risk to win?

Remember that the Chariot was originally an instrument of war. It guaranteed speed and surprise. With speed and surprise comes a certain amount of unpredictability. Accordingly, the Chariot predicts success and triumph. But it suggests competition, aggression, and haste, as well.

So, if it turns up in your reading, what does it mean? On the whole, it's a positive card. When I see it, I think of a winner, someone who put (or will soon put) everything on the line in order to achieve her goal. Very likely she will achieve it.

But you should be aware of some downsides. The card can suggest that some of your motives may have been less than admirable. Did you want to win? Or did you just want to beat the crap out of your opponent? There's an element of vengeance and belligerence to this card. Ask yourself: Have you been guilty of road rage?

The other downside is speed. In your rush to get where you wanted to go, you may have overlooked some important details. Or important people. If you're currently working on something important, and feeling, "Must finish on time," don't rush. Do the job right, that will impress the powers that be far more. If you're back in the dating game, don't throw yourself at the first guy who comes along. Maybe your career is your obsession right now—could your loved one feel neglected? Maybe your loved one is obsessing you—are your friends feeling neglected?

One consistent message of the tarot deck is the importance of balance in your life. Don't sacrifice everything at the altar of ambition or passion. The Chariot affirms that aggression is a normal part of life; if you *always* worry about behaving meanly or selfishly, chances are, you'll be unable to pursue the things you want. But hostility and injustice have a way of coming back to haunt you in very nasty ways. When you see this card, weigh the risks you're taking to win. You may find them perfectly acceptable. If so, full speed ahead.

Remember: slow and steady also wins the race.

THE CHARIOT REVERSED

Ooh, this is a frustrating card. Just when you think you've reached the finish line, your horse bolts in the wrong direction. You go ass over teakettle, you've wrecked the Chariot, and you wonder, "What the hell just happened?"

The Chariot Reversed represents failure of a particularly annoying kind: sudden and unpredictable. Things seem to be going along fine, and then everything collapses into a big steaming pile of ka-ka. People who get left at the altar probably would have gotten this card, had they thought to do a reading before the wedding.

This card doesn't offer a lot of comfort. Hopefully, it turns up in the past. If it does, be aware that this kind of upset can leave you unnecessarily skittish when it comes to commitment. If it occurs in the future, steel yourself now. At some point, you're going to be facing a pretty tough roadblock. Either think of how you can get around it or ask yourself, do you absolutely have to go down this particular road?

Honestly, you probably won't have much control of this situation—except in one area. The card suggests a failure to face realities. Realities that you can control. Look at the "Hopes and Fears" card in your spread. Do you have reasonable expectations? Would you define "failure" as anything less than absolutely perfect? In that case, you are destined to see the Chariot Reversed in many a reading.

STRENGTH

"You gain strength, courage, and confidence by every experience in which you really stop to look fear in the face. You are able to say to yourself, 'I lived through this horror. I can take the next thing that comes along. . . .' You must do the thing you think you cannot do."

—ELEANOR ROOSEVELT.

On the surface, Strength seems like a pretty straightforward card: You're strong. You can handle it. You think of stiff upper lips and bench-pressing things. You're tough, you've got what it takes (whatever "It" is: Life, presumably). If you see this card in a present or future position, you can expect a time of energy, courage, and confidence. You will take action, stand up for your convictions. You may even roar a little. That's fine.

But what is strength, exactly? As most of us have discovered at those times which require it, strength is not at all simple or straightforward. Would that every problem could be solved by lifting it above your head, then tossing to the ground. Maybe you'd like to try some Wrestlemania moves on your boss/boyfriend/entire family. But will making your guy scream "I'm your bitch" really address the issue?

Many of us eschew Wrestlemania and move straight to Stiff Upper Lip. "It's okay, doesn't bother me. I could not care less." Lies, all lies . . . but, hey, as long as we put up a good front, right?

The Rider-Waite image of Strength is a woman leading a lion by what seems to be a daisy chain. O . . . kay. It becomes clear if you know that the lion represents passion. In other words, our heroine has tamed the beast and now leads it around like some tabby cat in search of Whiskas. No whip, no chair, no chains; no animal was harmed in the making of this image.

It took strength to confront the lion. Strength is not freaking out, even though you want to. Strength is not pretending the lion isn't there and doesn't have to be dealt with.

Let's say the lion represents a difficult situation. Most difficult situations involve strong emotions. As we know, because we are not three years old anymore, Life isn't fair. You lose jobs, loved ones—things and relationships that matter to you.

But you can control yourself. When the shit hits the fan, and you want to start screaming and crying, stop. Two things are not helping this situation: rage and fear. They can devour you. You need to get those feelings under control. And not with a blunt instrument, but with calm, reason, and detachment. This card is also called Fortitude. What exactly is fortitude? I looked it up. It is what allows us to get through adversity with courage and a certain amount of dignity.

In other words, strength.

STRENGTH REVERSED

There are two ways you can be . . . unstrong. The first is obvious: weakness, hesitation, division within your own mind or the group you have to work with. The second is to abuse your power.

This, unfortunately, is not a card of moving forward. What you want to see in your future cards is a sign that you will possess the will, luck, or timing to make a significant change or improvement in your life. If you see Strength Reversed in a future position, it's unlikely you will—at least, in a positive way.

But, as always, it's instructive to look at what might be holding you back. In one scenario, you simply lack the resolve, or ability, to get what you want out of your situation. Nerves might prevent you from asking your boss for a promotion, or you may be a poor candidate for a promotion. Only you know which it is.

Or, in the second scenario, abuse of power, you may storm in, demand the promotion, say you will quit if you don't get one . . . and you may get one, because, in the busy season, the company can't afford to lose you.

Well, cool, you say, I win. Except, not really. Coerced advancement never really works. In a year, when that raise doesn't seem like much, you'll be in a poor position to demand more, because your boss will quite rightly say, "Hey, we just promoted you, time for someone else to get a break."

Same with romance. You've decided you want a relationship but, as we know, you have all sorts of ways to sabotage yourself in *l'amour*. You can radiate self-doubt and insecurity, you can allow yourself to look or behave in ways that turn off suitors. Or, you can come on so strong that all but the most masochistic run for the hills.

Or, say you're in a relationship, and you want something to change. You want your loved one to . . . be kinder. More ambitious. Do more things with your friends. You can either be passive-aggressive and never say outright what you want, all the while fuming that the Loved One isn't getting your oh-so-obvious *hints*! Or you can force the issue in a negative way, which will probably result in misery and resentment for all.

So, how do you avoid all of the above? Tough question. Be aware of the potential drawbacks of your approach. Try to be as firm and rational—and fair!—as possible in your dealings. Then last, but not least, realize that no one is perfect, and if you screw up, the world won't stop turning.

THE HERMIT

"*Blessed are the ears that are attuned to the soft whisper of God's voice and ignore the buzzing of the world.*"

—THOMAS À KEMPIS

One of the first questions that arises with the Hermit is, who's doing the hermiting? Have you retreated from the hurly-burly of life to gain peace and insight through solitude? Or will some mystical old guy impart his wisdom to you?

I will admit my prejudice here and say I just don't see too many wise counselors around these days. When I see the Hermit in a reading, I generally see it as a time of withdrawal and reflection on the part of the questioner. Even if you're seeking help from a therapist, or your higher power, you're also pulling back from the noise of daily life and seeking perspective.

For some people, this may indicate an actual journey, getting away from it all in the most physical sense. For others, it may just mean withdrawing mentally and emotionally. Canceling a few thousand dates. Not being available when Mr. Wrong calls. You haven't made up your mind to dump him, but as you mull it, you don't want to be distracted by his bullshit promises.

In the work realm, it can mean a sabbatical. Or, it can mean not joining in all the lunchtime moan sessions. Sure, they feel good, but do they really get anything accomplished? Do they help you figure out what to do next? If not, dispense with them.

There are aspects of self-denial in this card, hints of fasting and exercises in purity. You may choose to cut out some of your crutches—excessive socializing, drinking, bitching. (It doesn't have to be an obviously negative thing. Too much work or over-involvement in a person can serve as a crutch, too.)

As, indeed, can solitude. The tarot reminds us that, while it's all very well to pull back from the flashier, more transient aspects of living, we must reengage at some point. This card hints at regression and emotional withdrawal, as well as elements of deception. Are you hermiting or are you hiding? Not committing more emotion and energy to a bad situation? Good. Refusing to deal with life? Bad.

THE HERMIT REVERSED

There are lots of meanings bound up in the Hermit Reversed but, essentially, they all come down to the same thing: bad judgment. If you find this card in your future, you might almost try doing the very opposite of what you had planned. That's how flawed your first impulse will be.

There are many ways to choose poorly. You act too hastily or too slowly. You're too aggressive or you're too cautious. Any one of these is available to you.

And, of course, since the Hermit Right Side Up represents a wise counselor able to dispense insight and illumination, the Hermit Reversed represents, well, a quack. The elements of deception present in the Hermit Right Side Up are *glaring* in the Hermit Reversed. You're not dealing with the truth and nothing but the truth in your current situation.

Are you relying on someone to guide you through your problems? If so, you might take a step back and check that this person isn't some kind of Linda Tripp, pretending friendship and planting daggers when your back is turned. It doesn't even have to be a treacherous situation, but someone may be giving you bad advice right now. There's something corrupt in your confidante situation.

If the card turns up in the past, it signals that you've made some poor choices. There's a reason you're not happy right now. Suck it up and try something new. *Don't* hook up with another bad boy; try Mr. Dull—you never know. *Don't* switch jobs over and over because you're bored.

I can't advise you to not make a decision until the danger time passes, because that, too, is one of the ways you can go wrong. Be very truthful with yourself about what you want to achieve and whether you're really going about it in the best way possible.

THE WHEEL OF FORTUNE

Round and round she goes,
Where she stops, nobody knows.

—ANONYMOUS

The Wheel of Fortune is one of my all-time favorite cards. It means you're in play. The game's afoot. Something—we don't know what—is going to happen. Whatever you've been dealing with will finally come to a resolution of some kind.

The Wheel of Fortune represents all those big fortune-telling words: Fate. Destiny. Outcome. And, if you're like me and skip ahead in books to find out what happens because you can't stand not knowing, this card is good news.

(But will it *be* good news, you ask? That, we do not know. That, we have to look to the rest of the cards to reveal.)

So, why do I love this card? Often, with tarot, you can get a slightly open-ended reading. You ask, Will I get back together with my boyfriend? And the cards might show you a scenario for love, rebuilding trust, and a young man who resembles your boyfriend in some way. That indicates a good chance that you'll experience some sort of reconnection with your beau. The cards usually don't say, *You will get back together with your boyfriend, and you will marry him, and you will live in bliss and harmony, until the age of ninety-five when you both pass away in your sleep on the very same day.*

That, the cards won't give you. That, frankly, you shouldn't even want. Life is too complicated for Big Answers in ten cards.

But when you see the Wheel of Fortune, the cards are telling you that this story has a definitive ending. Something *will* happen. Back to our boyfriend and breakup scenario: If you see love-and-trust cards throughout the reading, and it all culminates in the Wheel of Fortune, then you can feel assured that rekindled romance is on the horizon. If you see doubt, fighting, and ugly-secrets-revealed cards, then the Wheel of Fortune probably means that you'll realize he's a dud and move on.

But, whether you like the outcome or not, the Wheel of Fortune means progress. Moving on. One chapter ends, another one begins, and so on.

And that's a whole lot better than being stranded in a quagmire of "If Onlys."

THE WHEEL OF FORTUNE REVERSED

★

You can interpret the Wheel Reversed in two different ways that are almost impossible to reconcile. I'll begin with the more common one, which also happens to make the most sense to me.

Sometimes, if the Wheel Reversed appears in your future, you can expect a stretch of bad luck. Whatever you hope for will be thwarted and delayed for a time. But, before you start busily trying to figure out what will cause all these mishaps, you should know that this is a particular kind of bad luck. It's the surprise, the unexpected, the thing you can't predict and, therefore, probably can't prevent. Whatever the bad break, it's very likely caused by an outside force that wreaks havoc at the last minute.

Some books promise that if you have courage, you will get your "happily ever after" in the end. Others are not as encouraging. But, because I don't want you to roll up in a fetal ball when all these mishaps occur, I will say that you certainly *won't* get what you want if you let these obstacles overwhelm you. That much is certain. Well, as certain as fortune-telling gets.

Now, for the less common definition, to which I wouldn't normally pay any attention, except that it happens to be Arthur Edward Waite's definition, and when he defines, we listen. Waite talks in terms of abundance and increase. This would seem to promise that your spin of the Wheel of Fortune would be a lucky one. But he also mentions superfluity, or too much of a good thing. It's hard to reconcile this vision with the others, but I bring it up because it is Waite, and because it's a lot nicer than hearing you're going to be experiencing a lot of hassle and headaches!

JUSTICE

"Justice is truth in action."

—Benjamin Disraeli

Does anyone actually believe in justice anymore? Aren't you convinced that the fix is in and the scum rises to the top?

A lot of the time, what happens in your life depends on the perceptions of others—your career advancement, your romantic life, how much mom and dad leave you as opposed to your loser brother who does nothing for them. The question that really pertains here is: Do others judge you fairly? If you show up and do the right thing, will you receive your just reward?

If you see this card in a future position, you can assume that, yes, you are operating in a realm of unbiased judgment and mature assessment. Justice presents an image of an impartial, reasonable, and incorrupt force in our lives. Other aspects of this card include balance, maturity, sound thinking, and clarity.

The card also suggests resolution—something you don't always get in tarot readings. If you see Justice at the end of your reading, you can be fairly sure your question will have a clear and fair outcome. (Please note: fair does not guarantee an outcome favorable to you.)

This all sounds good, doesn't it? You work hard, so your boss will promote you. You've spiffed up your wardrobe, gotten a fab new haircut and contacts, so you will get sex. You have braved auditions, and so you will get a part . . . .

We've spotted the disconnect, haven't we? Your own individual effort doesn't count for everything. Judgment, even fair judgment, is prone to subjectivity. We can hope for the will and the energy to do our part, and that the Cards of Fate aren't completely stacked against us by the boss's nephew, or that sly hussy men find inexplicably hot. This card represents, not a perfect world, but a just one.

JUSTICE REVERSED

You knew it! You knew the fix was in!

Say this for Justice Reversed, it confirms all your worst suspicions about how the world works. Whatever your situation, the forces of bias and prejudice conspire against you. Someone is abusing your trust. Bigotry and intolerance and favoritism loom. You're getting the fuzzy end of the lollipop, otherwise known as "the shaft."

The good and bad news here is that your current problems are not your fault. People are being "unfair." To some of us, this comes as an immense relief, as it lets us off the hook. The downside, of course, is that you're stuck in a situation in which you don't have total control.

So, how to get control? Well, first you have to figure out the problem area. Where do you feel particularly thwarted? If you're currently experiencing difficulties with your loved one, it may mean his moods and 'tudes derive from memories that have nothing to do with you. Is he confusing you with mommy? An ex-girlfriend? Time to point out that you're not them, thank you very much.

If the problem is work related, try to see if there's an issue of favoritism. Does your boss just "feel more comfortable" with your male colleagues? Has a new regime taken over and, for whatever reason, they just don't value what you have to offer? Can you live with it? If not, either confront or move on. But, by all means, don't blame yourself. It's their loss.

THE HANGED MAN

Not less I deem that there are
  Powers
Which of themselves our minds
  impress;
That we can feed this mind of ours
In a wise passiveness.

—WILLIAM WORDSWORTH

There's one very important thing to remember about the Hanged Man: He is not hanging by the neck. Traditionally, this card shows us a young man who's hanging upside down by one foot; he looks like he's performing a circus trick: the one where you go into a mystic trance, shrink yourself to half your size, and wriggle out of your bonds. He has not been caught, judged, and executed.

I point this out because, for some people, the Hanged Man represents a state of passivity that feels like death. It's a time of suspension, change, readjustment. It can feel like nothing is happening, and isn't that frustrating? Or, it can feel like so much is happening that you must give up all hope of controlling events and go with the flow.

And isn't that frustrating?

As a teen, I hated getting this card. I always wanted to be out there in the world, making things happen. To hear that I was not in control was maddening.

We have all had our Hanged Man periods. They come on slowly, make us uneasy and, invariably, lead to something better. It's that long stretch of boredom at work, the one where you feel you've done all this a hundred times before. Maybe you should quit, move on. But you feel unsure what to do next. It's the blah time in a relationship, the point where you may have realized your beloved is not going to change something he or she does not want to. You've stopped nagging them about it, which is good. Now you ask yourself, Okay, what next?

It can feel like depression, The Hanged Man Period. Nothing that really matters seems to be happening right now. A thousand petty demands that don't matter much to you clutter your life. Whatever the scenario, you feel the universe isn't very focused on your needs right now.

But you're wrong. Just because you're not boldly leaping into the next stage of your life doesn't mean nothing's happening. This is the lull before a significant change. Your unconscious mind needs time to work things through. The way to make yourself truly miserable is to not give it the time it needs. Fretting and struggling will get you nowhere. The thing to do now is calm down. Breathe deep; almost trance-like.

Shrink yourself down to half your size . . .

Then wriggle free of your bonds.

THE HANGED MAN REVERSED

Oh, it is just all about *you*, isn't it? You've built a little altar in your brain and placed you, wonderful you, at the center. No wonder you can't think of anything else.

If the Hanged Man represents a level of wisdom that acknowledges that your actions don't keep the world turning, the Hanged Man Reversed represents a level of narcissism that leads you to believe you're too important to bother with some things and too important to be left out of others.

If you see this card in the past, ask yourself if you failed to come through for someone. Sure, you told yourself you were too busy, the person wasn't that close a friend. Sorry! Cards say you behaved like a selfish jerk. Go directly to jail, do not pass Go, do not collect two hundred dollars.

Conversely, you might also ask yourself if the words "a tad pushy" describe you lately. Maybe you thought you were helping but, frankly, you were pushing in where you weren't needed, and made everything worse.

The fact is, you've been a bit blinkered recently, and you need to stop and remind yourself that the sun rises and sets without any help from you. Obviously, if you see the Hanged Man Reversed in the future, you can anticipate going through a time when you're going to be very "Me-Centered." This could mean acting like a lazy, childish slob. But, even if you're dedicating your time to others, you probably just want to see yourself as Mother Teresa for a little while.

Now, of course, there are times in life when we have to focus on ourselves in order to move forward. But this probably won't be one of those times. The Hanged Man Reversed predicts nothing positive. Words like "useless" and "unnecessary" abound in the definitions. Let life take over. Listen to others. Do *not* assume you know best.

DEATH

"Death is the privilege of human nature,
And life without it were not worth our taking."

—NICHOLAS ROWE

Let me begin by saying this: The Death card does not mean you will die in a plane crash next week.

Or a car crash, or a brain hemorrhage, or whatever your particular nightmare happens to be.

Death doesn't *mean* death. I've said it hundreds of times to people in readings and I've never been wrong. Not one of them has dropped dead, so far.

The reason that the Death card does not mean Death is that tarot has a particularly spiritual view of life and death. The extinction of the body is a metaphor for the liberation of the spirit. You pass out of this world and into the next. One life ends, true, but the next one is just beginning. However, let's be honest. The Death card represents transformation, and that can be a painful business. Change, real change, always means loss of some kind. If you see this card in your future, there's probably a major life shift coming up and it will probably involve loss.

I can remember two significant times this card came up in reading. One was my friend who was going to Paris to live with her boyfriend—only to discover that the boyfriend was cheating on her. (See Strange but True Tales of Tarot Number One: The Friend Who Went to Paris.) Bang. There went her dream of romantic paradise—along with a good chunk of trust and self-confidence. Loss, Death had predicted, and loss it was that came to pass.

The other time was when the company I worked for was sold to another corporation. I did a reading to see what my future held. The Death card showed me I wasn't going to be working there long, and it was right. The new corporate culture was completely different; the company I had loved working for was effectively dead, and I had to move on.

Both these experiences fall into the Life Sucks category. In my friend's case, she did move on to other relationships. But that experience affected her deeply, and probably caused her to make some poor choices later in life.

In my case, I would probably never have left that job unless I was forced to. Leaving it gave me the freedom to pursue writing full time. I loved that job, but I wouldn't trade the one I have now to get it back.

So. While there's no need to take out life insurance, you ought to prepare yourself for a big shift in your life. It may be painful; all reminders of our limited control over our lives are. It could be financial loss, illness . . . and, yes, maybe even a death. I can't exclude actual physical death completely. *But it has never happened in my experience.*

If you do get this card, don't fret. Fretting won't make things not happen. Focus on the afterlife instead. Truly, it can be quite glorious.

DEATH REVERSED

If you're the risk-averse type who thinks that sudden change is just about the worst thing that can happen, pay close attention.

Death Reversed does not promise change. "Whew," you say. It predicts dullness, inertia, stagnation. It's a mastodon stuck in the mud and drowning. It's Sleeping Beauty—only she never wakes up.

Chances are, if you're doing a tarot reading, you're not perfectly happy with your present situation and you'd like to be doing something else. You're not getting nooky, and you want some. You loathe your current job and wish to take up skydiving for a living. Your parents drive you crazy and you'd like to know if they're moving far, far away from you any time soon.

If you get Death Reversed in a future position, the answer is . . . no. Wherever you are, that's where you're going to be for a while. It's a jail sentence of a card. At best, there will be a slow, cautious modification. If this is the only kind of transformation you can handle, then fine. Death Reversed may be just what you want.

But whatever you want to say against Change, it engages you. Your senses are heightened, your mind and emotions are probably working on overdrive. Some people become addicted to this feeling and live their lives in chaos. We don't want that.

But we don't want to be sleepwalking either, going through the motions, not really caring one way or the other about much of anything. Sometimes, we're so far under we don't even realize it. We think this is just the way life is.

And so it is . . . when you're depressed.

Death Reversed can not only tell you you won't be making big headway on things any time soon, it can also serve as a wake-up call. Is this really the life you wanted to be living? If not, what can you do to change things?

The answer can't truly be "Nothing." This is your life we're talking about.

TEMPERANCE

"Temperance, sobriety, and presence of mind . . . are species of courage."

—Spinoza

Strangely enough, Temperance gets very little respect in the modern world. We may do yoga in order to achieve balance, harmony, and a better butt, but in truth, we secretly admire the driven, the frantic, the extreme.

Temperance is something the modern female needs to make a part of her life. It indicates everything you think it would: moderation, self-restraint, calm. Oh, let's go out on a limb and call it maturity.

So, what does Temperance *mean?* you shout. Well, if you've been feeling a little overextended lately, and you see this card in the future, it can mean you're about to approach life with greater economy. This can mean anything from putting yourself on a frugal—not crippling!—budget, to choosing a sensible diet as opposed to purging for two weeks.

In the workplace, it can mean the ability to work well with others, the ingenuity to adapt to rapidly changing situations. This woman does not sulk in the bathroom, bitching with her coworkers about how the new management sucks. This woman knows they suck, but the consummate professional, she makes it work anyway. (Maybe she's looking for a new job while she makes it work, but she doesn't let rage get in her way.)

In relationships, it represents a balanced union, one in which both parties give and take in just the right amount. No screaming. No yelling. Everything worked out in a calm, rational fashion. Doesn't sound very sexy? How sexy is crying and slamming doors after a while? Anyone who's been going through a rocky phase in their love life will welcome this card.

Self-restraint, frugality, patience . . . these are dirty words in our society. But take note: when you are centered, you are in control. You're acting, not reacting. Restraint may sound dull. But consider the alternative. Giving yourself away to anyone who makes demands or shows an interest—until there's nothing left?

TEMPERANCE REVERSED

Now you might expect that Temperance Reversed represents some wild party girl who's always two drinks up on everyone and likes to snap her thong in public.

If so, you haven't understood the true meaning of Temperance. Temperance brings just the right amount of yourself to the party; contributing, but not imposing. Temperance creates a level of harmony as everyone checks their egos at the door.

Temperance Reversed however is the rule of the Diva. Egos running amok. Argument. Discord. Mistrust. If Temperance Reversed turns up, know that you're in for a rocky time in any area of your life that involves other people. If you're trying to sort out relationship issues, you might want to play it cool for a while. This card calls for storms in the foreseeable future. Petty squabbles and turf wars could dominate in the office. Your family will suddenly disintegrate into a howling hydra of discontent. No one will communicate with anyone. Discussions will swiftly devolve into name-calling and bickering. It is not a good time to try and work anything out.

Don't even try to figure out who's to blame here. Right now, you'll probably only see things from your point of view and wonder why everyone else is behaving like a selfish asshole. Just sit tight and wait until everyone seems a little more rational. Then, maybe do another reading, and if the coast seems clear, start the dialogue again.

THE DEVIL

The day the devil comes to getcha
You know him by the way he smiles.
—Laurie Anderson

How does the Devil get you? Simple. He uses his credit card.

He buys you. Or you sell yourself. At some point, you gave your consent.

Remember this, because the Devil is a truly frightening card. Death at least offers hope of a new life. Not the Devil—or at least, it's not the kind of life you'd enjoy, although you may have thought so when you signed on the dotted line.

The key word to remember with the Devil is bondage. Enslavement to a power that cares nothing for your physical or emotional well-being. Think of addiction. The party-hardy drinking life seems like fun, at first. Until you start losing jobs because you can't function, relationships because your loved ones prefer you sober, and all sense of yourself apart from the damn bottle. But the bottle doesn't care. It's going to keep running your life until it ruins it.

Another useful analogy is an abusive relationship. Truly abusive. Someone who hurts you physically (in which case, put down this book and go get help now) or belittles you to the point where you no longer believe you have any power or right to stop them. You hope that they're in a good mood when they come home, and you say nothing to provoke their wrath and scorn. This doesn't have to be a spouse, by the way. I have known people lucky enough to have parents who treat them like this.

The abuse doesn't have to be current, either. If the memory and the bad lessons (i.e., you're a piece of shit) still have their hold on you, you've got trouble. Why do you think they call it wrestling with your demons?

Some people interpret the Devil as enslavement to the world of materialism. Obsession with things. Wealth. Status. In this case, the whole world becomes your keeper, as you rely on the opinions of others to propel you higher and higher and keep that money coming in. You have no time for a personal life. You don't even know who you are anymore—until you look at the fab flat screen TV, the Rolex, the BMW, and think, Oh, yeah, I do exist after all.

The Devil can mean other, bigger Bad News things. He can represent violence, a shock, even a death. He can indicate a human being who has a malign influence on your life, someone who encourages you to indulge in your worst habits. It can be that extra one hundred pounds you're carrying, or the jealousy that makes your life seem worthless—no matter what you may achieve, it won't be as good as what *she did!*

If this card appears in a significant position in your reading, do not freak out. You shouldn't decide that your boyfriend abuses you because he says mean things about your friends, or that you must lose ten pounds or you'll die. Think seriously about areas of your life where you have lost control, which are endangering your well-being.

As I say, the important thing to know about the Devil is that he requires your cooperation. He can destroy you, but he needs your help. He can't do it without you!

THE DEVIL REVERSED

It is extremely difficult to extricate yourself from a bad situation. Even when you know you have to get out, it can be hard to summon the energies and resources to do so. It's so much easier to go along, wait for fate to intervene, or hope that you can somehow just get used to it.

But if you see the Devil Reversed in your future, then you can look forward to that morning when you wake up, say, "I've had it," and take that first step toward changing your life.

If you get this card in your present positions, then you're right in the middle of that change. Needless to say, life is a little chaotic and uncertain right now—although, probably quite exhilarating. You'll have to follow your instincts for a little while. Look at the rest of the cards in order to find out what can help you or hurt you in your progress.

The Devil Reversed represents liberty, throwing off the shackles, releasing yourself from the ties that bind. Someone or something has finally pushed you that step too far. Or, maybe you complained to a friend, and they said, "I don't want to hear this anymore. *Do* something and stop bitching." It's whatever encourages/shames you into getting help, or getting out, or both. Bondage can take so many forms in this world of ours, as can the means of liberating yourself. The Devil Reversed can mean going into rehab, quitting your job if you feel stuck, or getting a job if you've been unemployed. It can mean leaving a relationship, or deciding you deserve a relationship. It represents changing the rules: you're nobody's patsy, not even your own, from now on.

THE TOWER

The ship. Great God, where is the ship?

—MOBY DICK

Two people fall from a burning tower under siege. The fortress, once so strong it seemed it could withstand anything, has been destroyed. A very potent image, the Tower scares most people because it represents sudden, cataclysmic change.

But not necessarily change for the worse. I'll explain in a moment.

The Tower, itself, suggests a sudden loss of stability and security. That could mean anything from a divorce, to bankruptcy, to an accident of some kind. This card symbolizes disruption, sudden breaks, and abandonments. If it comes up in the future, you will likely sever ties of some kind. The extent to which you initiate the change is not clear; but even if you're the one who calls the lawyers, you'll probably feel scared. No one likes this kind of change. Most likely, the event, whatever it is, will have you feeling like you're in free fall.

Now for the good news. In my tarot-reading experience, the Tower can suggest a violent, but necessary, break with something that held you back. Old fears and self-limiting assumptions, for example. A job that felt secure, but didn't challenge you. A relationship long past its expiration date—or destructive patterns in a relationship.

One of the most powerful readings I ever did was for a couple who were trying to decide whether or not to live together. (See Strange but True Tales of Tarot Number Two: The Man Who Fell Down the Stairs.) They both had big commitment issues. The Tower came up in their reading, and I thought, Uh, oh. Break-up time. The fact that other cards indicated love and happiness I saw as both of them moving on with new partners.

Wrong!

Right after I did the reading, the two went on vacation. First night of the vacation, he falls and breaks his hip. Qualifies as a calamitous event in my book.

But, because he broke his hip and lived in a building with no elevator, he had to move in with her. Basically, circumstances forced these two to co-habitate. And guess what? They found it worked a lot better than they thought it would.

The Tower, in this case, was fear. Tearing that Tower down—it's a very good thing. Still painful, still bewildering because you've lived with those fears and assumptions for so long. But, boy, it feels better once you're no longer . . . shall we say, imprisoned, by them?

THE TOWER REVERSED

The Tower Reversed represents inertia, oppression, same old same old, and the same old shit. In other words, you're in a bad situation, and if this card turns up in your future, you won't be getting out of it any time soon.

The sour relationship. The dead-end job. Financial debt. Envy. A past issue. The apathy and depression that keeps you from doing any number of things you know perfectly well you need to do—the Tower Reversed implies all these scenarios.

Question: Is someone trapping you, or are you trapping yourself? Most of the clues indicate you're slamming the prison door all by yourself. (Though some do admit you may be caught in a mess not of your own making.)

If you see this card in the present, you know you're living in a less-than-perfect world right now. You're stuck. Your mission, should you choose to accept it, is to figure out how you got there, and how you can get out of it. In this case, the distant past card is particularly illuminating. What old drama might you be acting out right now? Look at the future cards as well. Do they give any promise of release? And do they hint how that might come about?

If you see this card in the future, know that, on your present course, you're not getting out of this soon. This sounds like bad news. But, again, look at the cards to tell you about your mindset. Are you too timid? Too aggressive? Is there a face card—a queen or knight— in there, someone who might exert undue influence? A reading is not forever, and it's not set in stone either. Alter the present, deal with the past, and you can change the future.

THE STAR

Hitch your wagon to a star.

—RALPH WALDO EMERSON

Here, I have to quote Arthur Edward Waite. Of the Star, he says, "The summary of several tawdry explanations says that it is a card of hope."

Then he starts babbling about the Great Mother, and the Sephiroth, and receiving her influx, and I don't think we need to go there.

Let's stay with hope. Several words follow hope on the list: faith, inspiration, bright prospects. All well and good. Whatever the subject of your reading, if this card appears in a future position, you know that circumstances will favor you. If you hope for a relationship, you may meet someone soon. If you're in a relationship and things have been rocky or uncertain, matters will take a turn for the better. If you're looking for a new job, doors will start opening. If you feel depressed, kind of blah, you'll feel renewed energy and optimism.

But one interpretation stands out to me, and that's "the proper balance of hope and effort."

Why does the Star symbolize Hope? Think of famous stars. Bethlehem, the North Star . . . they serve as points of destination, guides. As long as you look up and see the star, you can feel optimistic that you're headed in the right direction, toward whatever the "promised land" means to you.

But you have to move your feet. That's part of the deal.

As we all know, it's very hard to get moving when you're bummed out. The Star addresses that. It gives you the courage to approach the cute guy in the supermarket. (It may even put the cute guy into the supermarket, who knows?) It drops a stray compliment from your boss's mouth, letting you know he values you, giving you the confidence to reach higher. It puts an *I Love Lucy* marathon on TV so you can laugh your way out of the blues.

However, if you don't do the approaching and the reaching, the *I Love Lucy* marathon is wasted. It's all very well looking up at the stars and sighing, "I wish." Take all this energy and inspiration and do something with it. Those "bright prospects" will start appearing real fast.

One last thing—Waite also provides an alternative, more negative interpretation of the Star. According to him, the Star can also represent loss or abandonment. He doesn't explain why, so I won't either. But bear in mind, those are possibilities.

THE STAR REVERSED

Understandably, the Star Reversed is a bit gloomier. Instead of all those hopes and dreams, we have disappointment and depression.

If you see this card in your future, you may not be getting what you wish for. As the old Gypsy might have said, "This is bad luck." You may find yourself thwarted on all sides.

Another aspect to the Star Reversed is stubbornness and arrogance. This could represent the person or agency to whom you're looking to make your dreams come true. They're not going to come through for you for whatever pigheaded reason. It could also, I imagine, refer to you, as you grow frustrated. When things don't go right, it's easy to get simplistic in your thinking: It's all their fault! There's nothing I can do! This mindset will only exacerbate your problems. Try not to give in to it.

Finally, there is another, separate meaning which I like to point out, and that is loss of a relationship. This could be a business relationship or a romantic one. This may sound like more bad news, but interestingly, one book defines the relationship as "unsatisfactory." It is usually scary to end relationships; there's always an element of anxiety entailed. However, if this relationship was unsatisfactory, it may have been the very thing that was blighting your hopes. So, whatever the pain and unease involved, you are right to end it, and will be better off in the long run.

THE MOON

"Everyone is a moon, and has a dark side which he never shows to anybody."

—MARK TWAIN

Forget any romantic notions of moonlight; here light is good because it lets you see what you're dealing with. Darkness is bad because creepy things hide in it. Cheating boyfriends, treacherous coworkers, or that shoe you left in the middle of the room, the one you trip over when you come home.

As a rule, you like to know what's going on. If the Moon turns up in the present or future of your reading, be afraid, be very afraid. You should hear Lassie barking a warning: Danger, danger! Where's the danger coming from?

Here's the worst part: You don't know.

The Moon represents deception. The unseen enemy. The whispering campaign against you at work. Nasty ulterior motives. The big smile on someone's face right before they stick the knife in your back.

It's the paranoid's card of choice.

The really tricky thing here is knowing what to do. Once you are aware of a perilous situation, the danger often seems greater than it is. You know how it is in the dark: every snapped twig sounds like a maniac coming up behind you with a chain saw.

Remember that, for the most part, the Moon represents the danger of human "truth." This card often depicts what people are saying: lies they're telling you, lies they're telling about you. Sticks and stones can break your bones, but names can never hurt you. And while lies may hurt, they don't kill you—well, not usually.

So, how to find the danger? Well, for one thing, make sure it isn't anything tangible, something like high blood pressure or any of those "silent killers." If you haven't had a checkup in a while, go just for the hell of it. Go through your financial papers; make sure everything's in order.

Finally, look at your own powers of denial. No one can deceive you like yourself. What problem are you avoiding? The Moon warns you that these problems will not go away simply because you ignore them. In fact, they rely on you to ignore them. The cheating boyfriend, the dad who drinks too much . . . they count on you being too frightened to say anything. So, you need to think. Hard. Talk things over with someone objective if you have to. And then, when you've separated the homicidal maniacs from the snapping twigs, pull a Buffy and kick their ass.

THE MOON REVERSED

Happily, flipping the Moon over lessens the danger of this card considerably. Deception and hidden trip wires remain, but they're much smaller and easier to deal with. In fact, you'll probably discover them before they do any damage. The Moon Reversed is petty secrecy, instability; irritating silences, but not deadly ones. Little lies, errors in judgment—don't worry, you'll live.

So, instead of the cheating beau, we have an uncommunicative one. Maybe he's never shared much, but your relationship has reached the point where it's become an issue.

Rather than your boss drawing up a list for the firing squad and putting your name at the top, things may just feel a little shaky at the office right now. Maybe it was a bad month in terms of sales, and that has everyone feeling nervous. Relax. Next month's sales will improve. The company will decide it's not a good time to lay people off (the tax benefits will be much better next year). Whatever. Instability prevails right now, but not catastrophically so.

Maybe a friend has gone incommunicado and you feel rejected. Maybe you underestimated your money needs for the month and now your wallet feels light. Maybe someone's taking advantage of you, and it's pissing you off but not enough to start screaming. Or maybe you're just going through one of your neurotic fits when nothing feels quite right. Not to worry. If you see this card in the future or present, you'll know that it's nothing you can't deal with.

THE SUN

Here comes the Sun, here comes the
  Sun
And I say, it's all right.
—George Harrison

Remember Snoopy doing the happy dance? That's the Sun. Basically, this card indicates everything good that could ever happen to you, from winning the lottery to world peace. You really, really want to see this card in your reading.

For the sake of clarity, let's try to define what kind of happiness this card promises. When I look at the Sun, I think abundance. Ease. Generosity. Enough love and material well-being to make even the most neurotic girl feel she can relax. Think of the sun as it must have appeared to your average medieval peasant—this wonderful brightness and warmth sent by God to banish the long winter and nourish your crops. You begin to get a sense of the expansive nature of this card.

Specifically, the Sun indicates success, but primarily in the area of the arts. It predicts a happy marriage, great sex, good communication, lots of laughs. You're generous, sensitive, a good friend. And why not? You're just so damn happy, walking down the street feels like a blessing.

The Sun primarily focuses on inner happiness. It concentrates on bliss that comes from your emotional and spiritual world: the arts, love, friendship. It tacitly acknowledges that the creditor banging at the door makes it hard to feel free and creative, but it doesn't promise wealth in the obvious sense.

With happy cards, there's never much to say. Which makes sense. Unhappy people, you'll notice, never stop talking. Bitch, bitch, bitch. Cut them some slack, they're trying to figure out why they're miserable. Happy people . . . well, they just sit back and smile serenely.

THE SUN REVERSED

There are two interpretations of the Sun Reversed: not as good news and bad news.

Waite believes that the card is such a positive card that even upside down, it indicates happiness and connection—although to a lesser degree. Maybe it's not marriage, but a first date. Maybe it's not complete success, but that first call back. If disappointment, it's only because your hopes were so high in the first place.

In general, the readings I've seen support the "bad news" scenario. This not a good card to get reversed if you're asking about a relationship, as it represents failure or disconnect in the romantic realm. Loneliness is specifically mentioned. If you were planning to officially hook up with someone—whether in the marital sense, or drunkenly declaring your love at a party—you should expect to run into a snag.

But how big a snag? How permanent the rift? Is this a time-out to rethink, or time to return the ring? Here, the Sun Reversed offers a ray of hope. It indicates the possibility of delay, as opposed to destruction. The future happiness you were striding toward with such confidence is now a lot less clear, but it hasn't disappeared altogether. Or, happiness may yet come, but it may be a lot different than you thought. So, later, you might look back on this time, and say, "Well, thank God I found out he likes wearing women's clothing *before* we got married!" As a result, you might have decided to forgo the match—or ordered an extra wedding dress, size extra large.

THE LAST JUDGMENT

"Don't wait for the last judgment. It takes place every day."

—ALBERT CAMUS

Many books choose to leave the "last" out, abbreviating the name of this card to Judgment. I'm leaving it in because, to me, this card is all about the link between atonement and personal growth.

The traditional image for this card shows Gabriel blowing his horn and the dead rising up, whole, happy, and joyous. In the simplest terms, the Last Judgment represents a reawakening, rejuvenation, renewal. It's a ruling in your favor, and according to some books, a positive event or outcome. So, if we're talking about a situation where you are to be assessed in some way and rewarded accordingly—a job interview, a first date—this card would indicate a happy result. It specifically mentions legal judgment as well as a promotion.

But let's get a little more serious. This card suggests the need for a sort of personal inventory. What can you change about the way you interact with the world that will leave both you and the world better off? Are there hatreds and resentments you're carrying around that you should let go? Patterns that you could change?

I don't mean to lay blame on the questioner. However, I don't think a reawakening just happens one morning over coffee. And sure, one welcomes positive judgment from on high—but isn't your own assessment of yourself important, too?

This card suggests a significant turning point in the life of the questioner. An "ah-ha" moment of clarity and resolve. A time when you are able to transform your life for the better. In the end, you must decide how you wish to interpret this card. You may rightly feel that it represents reward for past efforts, karmic payback, so to speak. Or it may speak directly to that part of you that's just a little fed up with things—and wondering what you can do to change them.

THE LAST JUDGMENT REVERSED

Judgment can disappoint in two ways: one, you don't like judgment and, two, judgment is postponed and you're left in limbo. The Last Judgment Reversed covers both these possibilities, and a few others.

Let's take the first: judgment you don't like. This could mean you don't get the job, the bank turns you down for a loan, or your first date thinks you smell. Whatever the opposite of "positive outcome" is, that's what we have here. Waite uses an interesting word: "sentence." This differs from judgment, as it implies you were found "guilty" of committing a certain action, and now you will discover the consequences.

Now on to the second: judgment postponed. This, in some ways, is a bigger drag. There's delay, indecision. People are hedging their bets. You'll hear the old "We're still interviewing" line or Mr. Dream Date telling you that he has a girlfriend, but he's breaking up with her . . . . Or maybe you've got cold feet and you're second-guessing all over the place. Weakness and wimpiness are elements of this card.

This card also contains an element of emotional or romantic disconnect. The word divorce is specifically mentioned in some cases. Someone is looking at you and seeing something they don't like or trust—or vice versa.

The lovely thing about the Last Judgment is its vision of rebirth and renewal. That, sadly, is lacking when the card is upside down. You're in limbo, baby, possibly even hell. The good news? Tarot readings aren't for eternity.

THE WORLD

And I think to myself
What a wonderful world.

—George David Weiss and Bob
   Thiele, "Wonderful World"

The World is the best and brightest of the good news cards. The final card in the Major Arcana, it predicts the strongest, most complete, and long-lasting changes. This isn't one happy day, or a lighter mood, or things getting a little better. This is huge, cosmic happiness.

As I've said, often tarot cards will show you incremental change, short-term results, or the early stages of your progress (or lack of thereof) toward a goal. If you're lucky enough to see the World at the end of your reading, it's the closest a tarot reading will come to saying, "Yep, you are getting what you wished for."

If you asked a *Will I fall in love?* question, you can think in terms of a genuine relationship. If you're wondering about an artistic endeavor, this card predicts a significant piece of good luck, a break that will have a real effect on your artistic life. If you're asking about career, you can anticipate locking into a job or a company that will fully utilize your talents—and reward you accordingly.

Success, change, fulfillment, completion, admiration . . . these are the specific words used to describe the happiness of the World. The card definitely has a "worldly" focus that might seem to preclude romance—but such a big, expansive card covers all aspects of life.

There are some interesting particularities about the success predicted, though. Waite puts the stress on a voyage, a change of scene that I think can roughly translate as a transformation of some kind. Either physically or mentally, you're making a serious change in your life (hence the reassuring totality of the card).

I've also seen the word "attachment" connected with this card, which I find interesting, primarily because I don't think isolation is conducive to happiness—or prosperity. Any successful, well-rounded life suggests a person connected to the world around her, drawing energy from them, and giving energy back. That's a tough balance to strike, as we all know, but it's essential, both in your intimate relationships, or your workplace.

Finally, the World represents the ideal balance of freedom and connection, of material reward and emotional stability, that state of inner peace and confidence that I will describe as being so self-assured that everyone finds you wildly sexy and attractive, even though you don't in the least match the *Vogue* standard of so-called beauty—and you don't care to. You're too happy and engaged to worry over other people's shallow standards of success.

All I can say is, "Congratulations."

THE WORLD REVERSED

If the World is a vision of an energetic life well lived, the World Reversed is stayin' stuck in your small town because you don't have the guts to get on the Greyhound bus and head for the big city. (Or, staying stuck in the big city because you don't have the guts to move to that small town.)

Inertia. Stagnation. Incomplete effort. The World Reversed connotes all these things. If you're hoping for a life shift of some kind, and this card turns up, you know you're either not dreaming big enough, or all you're doing is dreaming. I see this theme in readings time and time again. You're letting fear get the best of you. You want big change, but you want it to just sort of happen to you. Dropping old patterns and habits, trying new things, risking rejection . . . God, that's *way* too scary.

The World Reversed is a very strong card, which means that it may be hard for you to effect the changes you need to. I say this not to wave a finger in your face, but to suggest you may need some outside help at this time. Counselor, therapist, whatever you want to call it. You could use an outside perspective.

There is, of course, an upside to all this failure to move forward: permanence, safety, consistency. You can take a certain comfort in knowing that if you never attach yourself to anyone, you won't lose them. If you never show your artwork to anyone, they can't say it sucks. If you shoot for the lowest possible rung on the career ladder, you'll never have to know what you can't do in life.

But that's not a life for you. Not for a brilliant, gifted, attractive person such as yourself. In fact, it's barely a life at all. You deserve better.

Get out there, find "better," and grab it. Then start looking for "great" and "fantastic," and grab them, too. In other words, turn your upside down World right side up.

Strange but True
Tales of Tarot Number Two

The Man Who Fell Down the Stairs

This reading turned out to be so eerily on target that the man who asked for it has never asked me for another one. It's a fascinating example of how good things can come out of truly rotten events.

He wouldn't tell me exactly what his question was, but I knew he and his longtime girlfriend (so long-term it's silly to use the word "girlfriend") were having some relationship issues, the prime one being: would they live together and, if so, where, as they currently lived in different states. They had gotten so tired of fighting about it, they decided to take a vacation.

The reading involved a lot of Cups, a suit that relates to heart and home, so I immediately guessed he was asking about family issues. It also indicated a journey. That would be the vacation. What I was really interested in was to see what would happen during and after the vacation. Would sharing a house for three weeks give this couple any insight on sharing a house on a more permanent basis? And, if so, what would they do with that insight?

The First Future card was the Ten of Swords. Not a happy card. Ruined plans. Unexpected misfortune. Pain, misery, tears.

Okay.

The Second Future card was also not reassuring. It was the Tower. Change, catastrophe, painful upheaval. Sure, enlightenment comes from change, but this did not look fun.

I thought, "Breakup time."

The Final Outcome card was the Six of Cups. Now this was a slight surprise. I didn't expect a card about nostalgia and childhood memories to turn up at the end of this gloom-and-doom reading. The card also indicates new beginnings and opportunities, going back to your roots to find out what really matters to you, and then starting fresh.

"Huh," I thought. "Old girlfriend from the past. He'll date her on the rebound after the breakup."

Now, of course, I couched all of this in very positive, affirming language. Yes, there was a lot of pain in the middle, but it all came out right in the end. Focus on the journey, not the pitfalls. Whatever. I mentioned nothing about breakups, because who needs me butting in?

And it's a good thing I didn't. Remember the Tower? Well, you may or may not remember, but in the image of the Tower there's a man falling.

On the very first night of their vacation, my friend fell down the stairs and broke his hip. You can break things to different degrees. This was a bad break. Lots of pain, long recovery period, intense physical therapy.

As my friend lived in a five-floor walk-up, there was no question of returning home. So, he moved in with his girlfriend while he recovered.

And I guess they must have liked it, because it's been more or less their status quo ever since. (It's been years now, so I feel confident saying this.) The accident forced them to acknowledge the real strengths of their relationship, instead of the differences which had been their main focus while fighting. My friend did meet up with a girlfriend from the past—his early vision of his current girlfriend.

So, there you go. Vacation from hell provides happy ending!

The Cards

The Minor Arcana

Cups

*W*hen I see Cups, I think of the heart. Cups represent the emotional and spiritual realm. If you ask a question about a romantic matter, you'll probably see a lot of Cups in the reading. It's the suit of love, domesticity, creativity—everything that grows in the unruly garden of human passion. It contains all those essential liquids of life: blood, water, and wine. Essential—and potent. Drink too little and you're limp and dehydrated. Drink too much and you're hung over. Balance is key.

FLOW, BABY, FLOW.

Ones are all about beginnings, fresh starts, first steps. So the One of Cups represents the start of something wonderful in the fullest, most spiritual sense. It suggests fertility, creativity, abundance.

This is definitely a card you want to see if you ask, "Will I get pregnant soon?" Or if you want to know if that nasty bout of writer's block will ever end. See this card at the end of a reading and you know it's coming—that first great day of writing when you've hit on something really special and the words flow just as fast as the benevolent muse can send them.

It's the first day at the office at a job you've wanted forever, the one that'll finally make use of all your talents and help you grow in ways even *you* never thought possible. It's that giddy feeling after Mr. Right asks you out. The morning after a great night's sleep when you bound out of bed, ready for anything. You're taking a leap, and you don't need a net because you can fly.

ONE OF CUPS REVERSED

PISSING ON YOUR OWN PARADE.

Okay, you goofed. Happiness was just around the corner, but fuming over something you heard on the radio, you missed the exit completely.

Good things surround you, but your head's too far up your butt to notice. You're letting your anxieties and material concerns cloud your judgment. Now, there's nothing wrong with paying attention to the facts of life known as money and status—unless they make you a joyless pill. Maybe you started that great job, but the pay annoys you, even though you're doing just fine money-wise. Or when that guy asks you out, you think, Well, he's *okay*, but he's not rich, successful, and beyond gorgeous. Obviously, you're settling if you date someone who's fun, sweet, and makes you feel totally yourself—right? Well, wrong, and you know it.

So what? says you. *All that's needed is a little head adjustment.* Sure, but have you ever tried to get back to that exit you passed on the highway? What a pain in the ass, right? Life's great moments fly by pretty fast—don't miss them.

TWO OF CUPS

IT TAKES TWO, BABY. . . .

Almost more than any other card, this is the one I like to see at the end of a reading about love. The Lovers are sweet, but there's an element of cluelessness about them. Romeo and Juliet *before* the trouble starts.

There's a reason that the Two of Cups can be about love *or* friendship; it suggests two working brains, two hearts capable of commitment and worthy of trust. This couple has an aura of depth and maturity. (Not boredom, gals, not settling! Don't confuse the two.) This pair works at things. They do fight, they do compromise, and it makes their bond much stronger. They are each other's best friend—but not that creepy Siamese-couple way.

This card could also indicate a creative partnership. A boss or a coworker who seems like a human being—a great person to bounce things off of, generate new ideas, fresh directions.

Or it could be about that woman you just met at your coworker's baby shower. When the two of you single gals sat in a corner, swigging champagne, having a good old time. Call her. She could be the friend who will get you through everything from the date from hell to a shadow on the mammogram.

TWO OF CUPS REVERSED

DAMN, YOU KNEW YOU COULDN'T TRUST THEM.

If the Two of Cups right side up represents maturity and cooperation, reversed is selfishness and betrayal. It predicts separation, a troubled relationship, even divorce. It's that sinking feeling you get when your so-called best friend starts hitting on your guy. Yeah, you knew she was like that, but you never thought she'd do it to you!

And, by the way, why isn't your guy telling her to get lost?

So, you're fighting. Arguments, blow-ups, sulks, and mistrust. But is it a real fight? Should you dump him? Or her? Or both? Two of Cups Reversed indicates a loss of balance. The power has shifted in the relationship. Someone's too needy or someone's withholding. Same cards warn you when your perspective is off; but when I see this one, I tend to place the blame on the other person. The relationship may not be lost forever, but you need to adjust your expectations. Prince Charming has feet of clay. Will new footwear fix the problem? Adopt a wait-and-see approach.

THREE OF CUPS

SWEET HARMONY.

This card reminds me of that moment when the last guest has left the party, and you can put your feet up and say, "Well, that went well!"

Basically, this card addresses the risk that occurs any time two or more members of the human family come together and try to do something—be it love, business, or a cocktail party. You're always nervous *something's* going to go wrong. People, being what they are, will screw up somehow.

Relax. See this card in the future and you can rest assured that it will all turn out fine. Harmony, happiness, and healing in one gorgeous hot bath of a card. If the parties involved have had problems, they will be resolved peacefully and maturely. Your divorced parents will come to the wedding, and they will get along *fine*. You and your beau have been squabbling—but this, too, shall pass. If it's in the past, it might refer to the essential foundation of the relationship, reassuring you that you're basically on solid ground even if things feel rocky right now.

THREE OF CUPS REVERSED

TOO MUCH OF A GOOD THING.

Your cup overfloweth—and right onto the carpet, too. If Three right side up is Happy Times, reversed is Hangover. You're overdoing it. This indicates the kind of frantic socializing that happens when you're terrified of being alone. You spent the night gossiping with the gals from work—only to wake up at two in the morning and think, "Oh, shit, I can't believe I told them that."

Or, it could represent socializing with an agenda. Networking. Making connections that have a lot more to do with liking what a person can do for you than, say, liking that person for themselves. Nothing wrong with that, but it is a little unwholesome. Three of Cups Reversed suggests that there's something a little insincere, a little immature, or just plain old icky, about the connections you're making right now. Maybe you have to make them. Maybe that's where you are right now. But don't mistake them for lasting, emotionally sustaining bonds.

FOUR OF CUPS

SPINNING YOUR WHEELS.

You're used up, exhausted, and just plain disgusted with everyone around you. This isn't just a hangover, this is What am I *doing* with my life? Maybe you've been partying too hard, maybe work has been *insane*. Whichever, you've been on the Narcissism Trail, and just how did you get so far down the wrong path? Yeah, it looked great at the time but, face it, right now your life has all the richness and appeal of burnt earth. (Or, burned-out earth.)

This card rings as loud and clear as a referee's whistle: Time Out! Cancel all those social engagements, tell your boss you're taking a long weekend. Kick off the high heels, scrub away the make-up. Sleep for about twenty hours. Then take a good long look in the mirror. Who is that woman? And what the hell does she want?

FOUR OF CUPS REVERSED

WASH THAT MAN RIGHT OUTTA YOUR HAIR.

You know the theory that you have only so much room in your life and that if you want to let something new in, you have to clear out the clutter? You've done the clean-out and now you're ready to move forward. The key word with the Four of Cups Reversed is *new*. New possibilities, new romance, new solutions to old problems.

If you're feeling depressed about something and you see this card in the future, take hope. You'll soon be feeling much better. Take a look at the cards around it to see what aspects of your life could be tossed. Unsolvable problems dragging you down? A relationship that wears you out rather than energizes you? Maybe you should leave the office at seven instead of eight-thirty?

See this card in the present, and you know you're in the right frame of mind to start something new. Is there a One of anything hanging around? Love or lucre—grab it. See this card in the past and it tells you that wherever you are now, you at least started off on the right foot. So what went wrong? Well, that's for the other cards to reveal.

FIVE OF CUPS

YOU CAN'T ALWAYS GET WHAT
YOU WANT. . . .

You've got the blues, you're crying into your beer. Right now, life just sucks. And your gloom-and-doom mood isn't helping.

Given the suit of Cups, we're probably talking about a relationship. This could represent a loved one or the whole damn world. The original Glass Half Empty/Glass Half Full scenario, this card traditionally shows a man weeping over three spilled cups. Some disaster happened here. Something has been lost. But he fails to notice the two cups still brimming full behind him. Now, if he isn't careful, he'll be so preoccupied he'll trip and knock them over, too. But right now, there's hope—if he could only see it.

This could apply to almost any situation, but will probably pop up most in Should I Dump Him? readings. When it does, it's a clear sign that you shouldn't give up. Take some time, get distance. Then, when you're feeling more rational, focus on what you do have with this person, and see if those two cups aren't enough.

FIVE OF CUPS REVERSED

But if you try sometimes, you might find
You get what you need.

—Mick Jagger and Keith Richards

If Right Side Up is loss, Reversed is recovery, hope, making new connections or reviving old ones.

Maybe *you* got dumped, but now he's back, saying he made a terrible mistake. Or after that awful fight—the one that convinced you it was *over*—you both got a good night's sleep, and now you feel ready to talk. Amazing how easily you can work things out once you stop screaming at each other.

Or, maybe, one relationship has ended, but now you've spotted someone new in town. Or, you've realized you will never hear your mom say she loves you most—and that's okay. Basically, now you can move on from the pain. And, everything will fall into place from that point on. Usually when people ask for a tarot reading, they feel pretty lousy. This card offers hope. It tells you, this too shall pass.

SIX OF CUPS

BACK TO THE FUTURE.

Nostalgia. Regression. Sentiment. This is the high school reunion card. The sneaking suspicion that only in your past will you find the source of true happiness. It's the guy who would never date you in high school, but maybe he will now that you're thin, successful, and fabulous. Part of you knows that's ridiculous—he'll be married or gay—but some part of us always wants to feel we *can* go home again. And that it'll be better this time, damn it.

Now, sometimes, this card can indicate just the opposite: new friends, new opportunities. Sound confusing? Well, not when you consider that often, confronting the past helps us to move forward.

If you see this card in the past or present, it indicates that memories play a heavy role in the issue on the table. You want to ask how those memories influence your point of view. Do they clarify, inspire, or distort? If it's in the future, it could mean that part of the solution lies in the past. Feeling screwed up and confused about something? Give mom a call. You never know, this time she could be right. She's only known you all your life.

SIX OF CUPS REVERSED

NOW YOU'RE WALLOWING.

Sorry, it's time to move on. The past is never as great as you remember—or as bad. If you see this card in a reading, it shows that there's something you've got to let go of. Crummy childhood? Lousy boyfriends? Join the club. It doesn't mean you get to throw a self-pity party.

This card could also represent disappointment with something or someone from your past. You have outgrown that college friendship—time to move that relationship to holiday-card-only status. Or, if you expect money from an inheritance, or a handout from your folks, it's going to be smaller than you'd hoped. That guy you secretly hoped to run into at the high school reunion? He is married or gay.

This card can also show you what lies ahead. It's the future, still misty and uncertain. Some things will work; others might not. But, if you've felt stuck in the same old, same old, and this card turns up in a future position, changes may lie in store.

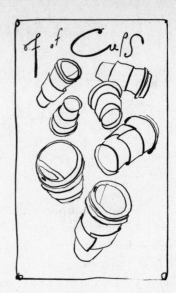

WELCOME TO FANTASY ISLAND.

Remember that game you played as a kid? The one that started, "When I grow up . . ." You were going to be an actress, have a big house, three cars, a gorgeous, totally faithful husband who's just a *little* bit less famous than you.

Then, as time went on, you grew out of that silly fantasy . . . right?

This card represents the imagination, wishful thinking, daydreams. If you see this card in the present or future, it may suggest you have somewhat unrealistic goals, whether it's the lifestyle of the rich and famous, or the perfect guy who has no flaws. You're stuck in the realm of dreams, unable to move on from childish fantasies of what life should be. We all have that friend who dwells permanently in La-La Land; she'll get this card a lot.

There's nothing wrong with fantasy. We all need it to get through life. What's the difference between a daydream and visualizing your goals? The willingness to get off your duff and make it happen.

SEVEN OF CUPS REVERSED

THE READINESS IS ALL.

If the Seven of Cups is all about getting lost in your daydreams, Seven of Cups Reversed shows determination, focus, and drive. You know what you want, and you're going for it, damn it. It's Mary Lou Retton pounding toward the vault, that look of crazed determination on her face.

If you see this card in the present, particularly in the central cross, it indicates that you're in a very good place to achieve whatever you want. Doesn't necessarily mean you'll get it, as we only control so much in our lives. But, whatever you need to bring to the table, you're bringing—with hot sauce.

See it in the future, and it means you will be getting to that point soon, which is good news. Look at the cards in between to find out what's disrupting that focus in the meantime.

EIGHT OF CUPS

DISILLUSIONMENT.
DISAPPOINTMENT.
DEPRESSION AND DE–SPAIR.

And what's really weird is, life's going fine. At least according to the outward signs.

The traditional image for the Eight of Cups is a man turning away from eight brimming cups and heading for the hills as fast as his sandals will carry him. If there were thought bubbles in tarot, his would read, "Screw this shit."

Maybe your high-powered job got a little too high powered. Maybe Mr. Wonderful, who everyone thinks you should marry, isn't all that perfect—at least not for you. Doesn't matter how great the whole world thinks your job, or your guy, or your life is—something is not working for you. You want something more. You may not know what that is yet, but you know you don't have it now. Stuff that seemed so important suddenly seems meaningless.

This card predicts a time of severe dissatisfaction. If you're asking about the health of a relationship, or their future happiness at a job, you don't want to get this card. Does the pilgrim find what he's looking for in the hills? We don't actually know. But we know he wasn't happy where he was. Maybe you should take a vacation. Maybe you should go into therapy. Either way, a change of perspective is in order.

EIGHT OF CUPS REVERSED

READY TO PLAY.

Eight of Cups Reversed is happy hour. It's energy, pep, zip. You feel up for anything. You're in a party mood. This card screams carpe diem.

Not surprisingly, this card also indicates a new love on the horizon. Because, as we all know, when we're feeling at our most fabulous and festive, we send out our most attractive vibes. Show off your plumage and someone's going to take notice. Maybe it's all a little frivolous, maybe a little shallow, but it beats feeling like shit.

QUEEN OF THE MOUNTAIN.

Ah, now here's the card you want to see with regard to any question about career. This is Success with a capital S and that stands for stock options. You fought your way to the top, you're playing with the big boys, and you're kicking their ass. It's about the image of success, too. The hard body, the connections, the ability to not only get a seat in the hottest restaurants, but the ability to look like you actually belong. Congratulations, you've made it.

Is there a catch? Not really. This is a happy woman, enjoying her executive toys and designer clothes. It's not really about fulfillment—although this person is quite content, thank you. It's about a certain kind of success, business and money-oriented. Granted, the money necessary to feather that lovely nest you've bought, crammed with all sorts of crass commercial goodies. But there's very little of home and hearth here. Better make a note in your PalmPilot: *Find domestic bliss.*

NINE OF CUPS REVERSED

HUMPTY DUMPTY HAD A GREAT FALL. . . .

Oops. You grabbed for the brass ring and fell off the merry-go-round. The Nine of Cups Reversed represents loss in the business area of your life. When you're about to go in and ask your boss for a raise, this is not the card you want to see. It's entirely likely that you not only won't get the raise, but that your boss will tell you, We feel you'd be happier somewhere else.

It's a lost wallet, a dip in the stock market. Or, it's blowing a week's salary on a pair of shoes that hurt your feet, but you're too embarrassed to return. It's too little or too much. Deprivation or indulgence. Either way, your sense of security and balance is thrown off. Everybody loves the winner we see in the Nine of Cups right side up; this person has to rely on her real friends. Maybe that's why this card can also represent truth and loyalty. When you're down, you find out what—and who—really matters in life.

TEN OF CUPS

THERE'S NO PLACE
LIKE HOME . . . .

Remember when I said there was something missing in the Nine of Cups? It's all here in the Ten of Cups. It's love, friendship, happiness, fulfillment, and a nice little house perfect for however many people need to be in it. This is a card you look for in a reading before a wedding or before relocating to a new town. Maybe you're starting a family; maybe you're starting a new life. Whatever you're embarking on, you can expect deep contentment and fulfillment in the personal connection area.

If the card is in the past, then you may be one of those rare people who had a happy childhood. This will naturally make you a much saner person than the rest of us. Or, if it occurs in the Hopes and Dreams position, it could refer to your expectations. Only the other cards can say if those expectations are realistic or not. If a lot of face cards appear in the reading, it indicates people taking a strong interest in your well-being.

TEN OF CUPS REVERSED

. . . AND SOMETIMES, THAT'S A GOOD THING!

This is not the card you want to see before joining your family for the holidays or going off with your beau on a vacation.

This card is all about people indulging their ugliest interpersonal impulses with no self-restraint whatsoever. Family strife. False friends. Petty quarrels turning ugly. If it occurs in the future in any reading about a relationship, beware: rocky times ahead. The person on whom you're focusing your energy—be it a lover or family member—may be untrustworthy. If it's in the past, well, hurray. Unless it's in the distant past, in which case you probably have major trust issues.

So, wise up about Mr. Wonderful. Skip the family reunion. Curb your own tongue—you don't have to say everything you think. Maybe if you act like a grown-up, you'll inspire those around you to the same.

PAGE OF CUPS

MAY I BE OF SERVICE?

The Page of Cups is essentially a card of service. Some interpretations specifically state that this represents someone who will help you. Be on the lookout for someone youngish, studious, and willing to work long hours. That new hire, maybe? Your landlady's handy nephew? Maybe he can get your toilet to stop running.

But this card could also indicate a phase during which you dedicate yourself to the task at hand, but not in a showy or dominant way. You may not be top dog, but you should win a lot of brownie points. You're not calling the shots, but you're in there, working quietly behind the scenes, and people have noticed. Or, maybe, night school is in your future, something that will help you reach the next rung.

Other possibilities for this card are the coming of news, or youthful arrivals, a.k.a. babies. Now, some will say this is a young man in your future. I'm personally wary of that interpretation, unless someone has expressly asked about romance; I don't get too literal about It's a boy in tights, must be Prince Charming! But if you do have your eye on that cute, bespectacled guy in accounting, go for it!

PAGE OF CUPS REVERSED

MYSELF BEFORE OTHERS.

That other guy was so sweet and reliable! This guy is a pain. He's flighty, determined to do what feels good and ignore those boring everyday gotta-do's. No sooner has he opened the textbook than a bunch of his friends entice him out to a bar for a beer. (Okay, several.)

This card is all about impulses and inclinations. If you thought you'd be buckling down and getting serious about something in the future, chances are it won't happen. If you hoped someone else would buckle down and get serious, the same thing applies. Don't expect that employee to tackle that stuff you asked her for weeks ago. Or, if you're wondering if your guy will ever grow up, it doesn't look good. He means well, but he's easily distracted.

And what happens when you call these charming loafers to account? They lie. Make excuses. Point fingers. This is also a card of deception. Even seduction. They get lured into messes, and they bring you right along with them. Fool you once, shame on them. Fool you twice . . .

Of course, if you're the grasshopper playing when you should be hoarding, well, *that* you can do something about!

KNIGHT OF CUPS

OPPORTUNITY
COMES A-KNOCKING.

Handsome guy on horseback comes bearing gifts. Sounds exciting, right? The Knight of Cups is exciting. He's news, a buzz in the air, that feeling that something big waits just around the corner.

Whatever it is that concerns you, there will be a development soon. A proposition is going to be put on the table, an invitation is coming in the mail. If you feel like you always have to work to make things happen in your life, now you can relax. For once, opportunity is coming to you.

If he is a guy, he's a real doll. Highly intelligent. And romantic. Into the arts, and he dances well, too. Met anyone like that lately?

KNIGHT OF CUPS REVERSED

DON'T ANSWER.

Remember the doll? Smart, romantic, great dancer? Did he sound too good to be true? He was.

Unfortunately, if this card is upside down, you may encounter something that feels like a lucky break, but you'd better read the fine print. If someone says, You could already be a winner! you're probably being conned.

So, this one time, listen to your neurotic instincts. That anxious little voice in your head that tells you this promotion sounds like more work for the same money; that the guy you met at the bar won't call, even though he swore he would—or if he does, he has a girlfriend. This time, someone really is trying to pull the wool over your eyes. So proceed with caution.

QUEEN OF CUPS

FOR HER PRICE IS ABOVE RUBIES.

The Queen of Cups is the Oprah of the tarot deck. Warm, loving, generous—and adored by all. She's gifted and talented, but she uses her skills to help others. She's everyone's dream mom, a devoted wife or companion.

What? Sounds nothing like you?

Well, that's why I called her the Oprah instead of the Earth Mother. Most modern girls don't identify with the serene hausfrau. It also doesn't do the Queen of Cups justice. Yes, she's all about the emotions and the heart and the home. But she's a really good friend, a terrific shrink, or the midwife who says, "Don't be dumb. Take the drugs."

On a less positive note, maybe she represents someone who's perfectly wonderful, but with whom you have a complicated relationship. Maybe she's the sister you feel you can never compete with. Or your mom, whom you adore, but on whom you rely a little more than a grown-up-type person should.

Or maybe you're just going to be very focused on home and hearth for a while. But, usually, the court cards represent an outside influence on your life, rather than a shift in your own emotional worldview. So figure out who the Queen of Cups is—and see more of her.

QUEEN OF CUPS REVERSED

DIZZY LIZZY.

Oh, God, we all know this girl. So warm, so sweet, she makes the best banana bread ever. But when you're getting together, always tell her an hour earlier than you actually want to meet. This gal is never on time. Not that she's passive-aggressive, oh, no.

She's got a weird, often oddly perceptive take on things. The moment you write her off as a flake, she says something that makes you think she's a genius. Probably an artist of some kind, she has a lot of dreams, but not much work ethic. And, by the way, can she borrow twenty bucks?

Don't ever rely on her. Also, the Queen of Cups Reversed doesn't age well. It's one thing to be a hippy-dippy chick in your 20s; by the 30s, it's like, Get a job, already. But if you value the relationship, don't let on. The minute she senses you getting judgmental or frustrated, she can turn hostile. She's reality-phobic, this one. The one time you'll ever see her really angry is when you wave a big cup of java under her nose and tell her to take a deep whiff.

KING OF CUPS

FAIR AND IMPARTIAL.

Each of the Kings has a different nature. This one represents professions or areas of life in which learning and intuition are key: law, the arts and sciences, academia, or the spiritual realm. Maybe he's a teacher who had a profound impact on your life. The rabbi who got you through your bat mitzvah. Maybe he's a judge presiding over your case about that annoying traffic ticket. If so, breathe a sigh of relief. He's fair, compassionate, and impartial.

So, why is he in your reading? Well, maybe he's having a strong impact on your current situation. Maybe he's a force for good you're overlooking. Or maybe he's just a sign that the universe is prepared to deal fairly and generously with you when it comes to your question.

KING OF CUPS REVERSED

THE FIX IS IN.

The jury's been tampered with. The judge is on the take. Whatever is going on, it's rigged against you. This could represent a case of outright fraud. Looking for a new apartment, take a very close look at that lease before signing. Just apply for a new job? Well, surprise, they have an in-house candidate and they were just going through the motions when they interviewed you.

What can you take away from this bummer of a card? Well, if it turns up in the past, present, or recent future, you know that if you suffered disappointment, or you suspect you're about to, it had nothing to do with you. It wasn't a fair fight and there was no way you could have won. If it's in the future, well, the King is pretty powerful. You can't force him to love you/give you the job/not be a crook. You may have to go elsewhere for what you want.

Pentacles

*P*entacles are all about cold, hard cash. They symbolize commerce, business, material gain—and loss. They're the Stock Market suit. Any reading about career, money, or your involvement in the larger world should involve a few pentacles. Interestingly, I have also seen pentacles feature heavily in several readings about love—a pretty good sign that someone's priorities were screwed up.

ONE OF PENTACLES

MONEY, MONEY, MONEY....

Remember that moment when Dorothy puts her dainty little foot on the first curl of the Yellow Brick Road? Well, if you squint a little so that the yellow brick becomes gold, as in "the streets are paved with," that's basically the moment here. The first step on the road to riches. This is a new job, a big raise, a move to the city and all its prospects. The inheritance that comes from out of the blue and finally lets you quit your rotten job and start that bakery you always wanted to. And you don't even have to be a greedy, heartless bitch about it. This card has a big-heartedness about it that means you're not exploiting anybody—including yourself—for financial gain.

ONE OF PENTACLES REVERSED.

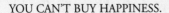

YOU CAN'T BUY HAPPINESS.

Oh, don't spit. Sometimes it's true. Think of your friend the lawyer who works a hundred hours a week. Sure, she makes a great salary, but what on earth can she do with it?

Money isn't everything. If you see this card in the future, you probably will have some money coming. (Phew! I hear you say.) But, beware, there are major strings attached and possible pitfalls to be negotiated. Maybe that inheritance does come through, and you do start that bakery. Did you check to make sure that your new space was up to code?

Or, maybe, the almighty buck looms just a little too large in your consciousness right now. Is the only lens through which you see your life colored green? Green for cash, green for . . . envy? Funny how those two always go together.

TWO OF PENTACLES

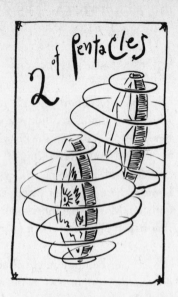

I'M DANCING AS FAST AS I CAN.

This is a very familiar situation for the modern gal. You've got a million things going. Every time you turn around, the phone's ringing, the e-mail's pinging, or someone's yelling, We need you right now! All very exciting and stimulating, but you're almost at the nervous breakdown stage. All is chaos and craziness, but *you* can hold it together.

Right?

Interpretations differ on the exact meaning of the Two of Pentacles. The traditional image of a young man juggling two pentacles suggests partying to some and busyness to others. I lean toward busyness but, whichever you choose, the theme is one of frantic activity, where you know people are just waiting for you to drop the ball.

If you see this card, it means you're either coming out of, or going into, a time of extreme engagement. Stretch yourself too thin, and problems will ensue, as this card also indicates difficulties, agitation, and embarrassment. No doubt you're telling yourself, No, no, I have to . . . (fill in the next one hundred blanks, but try paring that list down to fifty).

TWO OF PENTACLES REVERSED

BREAKING POINT.

You're still juggling frantically, but the balls are starting to drop. Or else, you're just going through the motions with a big, fixed smile on your face. (You know, exactly how the guy in "The Scream" looked right before they painted the picture.)

The Two of Pentacles Reversed can represent several things, from literary talent, to sending a message, to faking orgasm. (Most books refer to this as "simulated enjoyment.") But, the point is, you're telling a story. How much that story diverges from the truth only you know. If you end up with a big bestseller, great! But if the difference between what you're showing to the world and what you feel is too great . . . that way madness lies. So wipe the big grin off your face and tell your boss/husband/friends to start contributing a little more because you've HAD IT!

THREE OF PENTACLES

YOU'RE THE TOPS.

Just when you think nobody appreciates all your hard work, your boss calls you into the office and says, "You're fabulous. We're promoting you and giving you a big raise."

This card is about rewards, riches, payment for services rendered. The vision is of an individual who has achieved mastery of her realm—be it fashion design, copyediting, or computer programming—and is now reaping the considerable benefits of her skill and hard labor. And, yes, it could also be that project you've been working on, on the side—your dream career as an actress or interior decorator.

If you've been working toward something, and you see this card in the future, take heart. Your efforts will pay off big time. And it's not necessarily money, although Pentacles are the symbol of filthy lucre. It could also include acclaim, renown, public recognition. But, you have to make the commitment. You won't win the lottery; it specifically refers to recognition of your work. So make sure you're doing your part. Do not slack off now.

THREE OF PENTACLES REVERSED

YOU JUST HAVEN'T EARNED IT YET, BABY.

Why doesn't anybody appreciate you? Why does *she* get a raise and you don't? God, you are so screwed over!

Well, actually, you're not. The fact is, you haven't been bringing much to the party lately. Come on, admit it. Haven't you been spending more time bitching than working recently? Have the words "They don't pay me enough to do a decent job?" crossed your mind? Hm . . . and you wonder why no one's coming through with the perks and promotions.

This is the card of mediocrity. Preoccupation with money over true worth. Sloppiness, half-assedness . . . definitely *not* being the best that you can be. And that goes for romance, too, in case that was your question. Nobody will spend big bucks or big emotion on a spoiled, self-pitying brat who stomps around saying, "I don't care."

Now, here's the good news. You have control in this scenario. So get over your snit fit and go back to being that high-powered (and high-maintenance) lady everyone knows and loves. You catch more bees with honey and all that blah di blah. And, if they still don't realize your true worth? You'll feel better anyway, I promise.

FOUR OF PENTACLES

GREED IS GOOD. EXCEPT WHEN
IT TURNS YOU INTO A JERK.

If I tell you that this card in a Future position means you may have
some money coming to you . . .

Still listening?

Just checking, because this card suggests that, lately, you're *all*
about money. Material matters dominate your life right now. Yeah,
the money's probably coming in, but at what cost? This card suggests
a limited life, an ungenerous person. Miserliness, selfishness, capital-
ism at its ugliest. Scrooge before Marley stops by.

So, while the Four of Pentacles can be good news, it indicates the
need for a reality check. Not to mention a few other checks, sent to
various charities in atonement for your greedy, money-grubbing ways.

FOUR OF PENTACLES REVERSED

THE CHECK IS IN THE MAIL. NO, REALLY. . . .

You're still thinking about money. But you're not getting it any time soon if this card turns up in a Future position. So, if you're about to ask the boss for a raise, your parents for a loan, or God above for a winning Lotto ticket, think again. The universe is not in the giving vein today.

You need to think in terms of delay or opposition. Money will come later—but not now. You say you need it *now?* Didn't your mother always tell you, three months' rent at least in the bank? Maybe you need to start saving a little for a rainy day, missy, because the clouds are gathering.

Or, you may suffer an actual financial loss of some kind. Your 401(K) takes a nosedive. The restaurant where you work is shut down for health code violations; you'll be out of work for a month. Or, you lose your wallet, just after withdrawing a large amount of cash. Your radiator blows minutes after your muffler—and then you ding your rental.

Bear in mind: this is a setback in your financial schemes, not an irrevocable disaster. You're deprived, not destitute.

FIVE OF PENTACLES

BLACK MONDAY.

This is *not* a card you want to see in *any* reading, but particularly not those regarding money or career. The Five of Pentacles means a serious financial setback, such as the loss of a job, savings, or affordable home. Perhaps none of those things will literally happen, but it indicates a loss of cash so severe it can take a toll on your mental, emotional, and physical health.

Interestingly enough, some interpret this card as representing lovers with nowhere to go. It can represent a mistress or illicit paramour. So, you can also look at it as a state of insecurity, of being outside the sanctioned realm (e.g., marriage, or the corporate world) and so more vulnerable to hostile forces. At any rate, it foretells some rocky times ahead.

FIVE OF PENTACLES REVERSED

DARKEST BEFORE THE DAWN.

All good runs come to an end—but so do all bad ones. You have to start getting lucky again someday, and that's what this card is about. Just when you think the universe has royally screwed you, the planets tilt, something shifts and, suddenly, things start looking up.

But happy days aren't here again—yet. Maybe you lost a job, and now you have a new one. If you think, *I don't love it, but it pays the rent*, that's exactly where you should be. Maybe mom and dad gave you a loan. You'll have to pay it back, but it keeps the creditors at bay. Maybe you just woke up this morning and said, You know what? I'm tired of feeling like shit. This card represents that small but crucial step back to prosperity. But you know full well, it's a long haul.

Now, I hesitate to mention this, but sometimes the Five of Pentacles Reversed is much the same as the Five of Pentacles—only worse. But here I'm choosing to look on the bright side, and emphasizing the more hopeful interpretation.

SIX OF PENTACLES

LADY BOUNTIFUL.

This card represents that utopian state of mind when you have, you share, and you receive in return. It's prosperity, generosity, kindness. Good karma of the first order. A spiritual potluck. Everybody brings something to the table, and everybody eats well.

The traditional image for the Six of Pentacles is a wealthy merchant giving alms to the grateful poor. So, if you see it in the future of a reading about money, it does suggest that financial success and comfort are in store. But, more importantly, it indicates a spirit strong enough to spread the wealth. You always said, If I get rich, I'll give lots of money to charity. Turns out you were telling the truth.

SIX OF PENTACLES REVERSED

SCROOGE.

The Six of Pentacles Reversed shows us the darker side of money: things given with selfish motive or things withheld. Avarice, greed, a sense of never having enough and wanting to hold on to everything.

If you are in the midst of financial negotiations—this is not a card you want to see. Bosses are not going to be generous with raises. There may be family fights over money. This card reminds me strongly of parents or relatives who use an inheritance to control their children. Money is a powerful thing, people use it badly. Be sure you are not one of those people—or under that person's thumb. If you depend on such a person, you should strike out on your own, no matter how hard it may seem. Sure, it'll be hard to give up the cash, but think what you'll get in return: independence, self-respect, all that good stuff.

SEVEN OF PENTACLES

WORKING FOR THE MAN EVERY
NIGHT AND DAY. . . .

The Seven of Pentacles is a tricky card. It represents labor, hard work, and growth—but the outcome of all this effort is somewhat in doubt. Is this a delay, a setback, a time for reassessment? Sometimes. Is it joy in the work itself, a state of flow when you're living totally in the present? Sometimes. This card can mean both.

Goal-oriented people find this card difficult. Perhaps it really comes down to how you feel about the journey. The card can suggest that the work is good, but you're not seeing the rewards. A lot has been sown, not so much reaped.

Other interpretations disagree, saying that the card represents progress and success. But it's not a jackpot kind of card. This is a working woman's card. Wealth can be yours, but it will take a lot of hard work, and the wealth you receive may be money . . . or the satisfaction of a job well done.

SEVEN OF PENTACLES REVERSED

CAUTION! SLICK ROADS!

This card is much clearer. Isn't that always the way with bad news? The Seven of Pentacles shows impatience, frustration, and the hasty acts that arise out of those feelings. "Oh, screw it, I have to make a change; whatever happens, it can't be worse than this."

Well, sometimes it can.

This person *hates* the journey; she often takes a big step in the wrong direction because she just can't sit still. If you see this card in a decision reading (should I quit? should we break up? should I get a radical hair cut?), be aware that you may not be making a well-informed choice. When that voice yells "Jump!" don't listen. Wait. Think. Then think some more. Ask yourself, can I change something gradually? Look at things in a different light? Then in a few weeks or so, do another reading. See if you get the green light to go ahead.

EIGHT OF PENTACLES

"Blessed is he who has found his work; let him ask no other blessedness."

—THOMAS CARLYLE

Anyone who's ambitious is not going to find this a very sexy card. It doesn't promise huge success, or wealth, or fame. It's a card for the craftsman, a person who takes deep pleasure in her own work. It's about doing something because you love it. People may pay you to do it, but not a whole lot.

The Eight of Pentacles could also signify the early steps in a new career. The bottom rung of the ladder. Working your way up. Paying those damn dues.

The good news is that it's good work. You're skilled. Diligent. Hardworking. You deserve to do very well. The bad news is, there's no guarantee of crass monetary reward. But, as they always say, do you love it enough to do it if no one pays you? If so, and you're doing it, that's happiness.

EIGHT OF PENTACLES REVERSED

"Diligence is the mother of good fortune, and idleness . . . never brought a man to the goal of any of his best wishes."

—CERVANTES

Nothing illustrates the value of the Eight of Pentacles like the Eight of Pentacles Reversed. Here, instead of the diligent, skilled worker, we have the lazy, opportunistic suck-up. Don't you *hate* people like this? People who sit around, thinking the world owes them everything? Who take credit for things they don't do?

Hopefully, this isn't you. Hopefully, this represents your obnoxious boss or coworker, in which case, all your rageful feelings toward them are perfectly justified. Get away from this person. They can only mean bad things for your blood pressure.

Now, be honest—have you been going through a slothful phase? Do you wonder where all those big ambitions you had for yourself went? You certainly didn't mean to stay in this crappy job as long as you have. So what happened?

Just guessing, but maybe you experienced a lack of nerve. You procrastinated, got by, did the bare minimum. Boring people work hard—brilliant people achieve without breaking a sweat. Yeah, right. Could it be—perhaps you're not quite as brilliant as you thought. Well, if you roll up your sleeves and get to work, I bet no one notices.

NINE OF PENTACLES

SOMETIMES, MONEY CAN
BUY HAPPINESS.

This is a nice card, a card you'd like to see at the end of any reading about money, because it presents a lovely picture of financial security. You could practically use it as a commercial for an investment firm. The popular image for this card is a woman tending her garden; sort of Martha Stewart, but much, much nicer. You can look forward to this sort of bountiful, serene existence if you work hard, save your pennies, and pay your premiums on time. It's *mature* success.

In other words, the Nine of Pentacles is not a Get Rich Quick card. It's not even necessarily rich. But it's secure. A level of financial well-being that enriches your life, rather than demands you spend your every waking moment making money. Now that sounds nice, doesn't it?

NINE OF PENTACLES REVERSED

But I do guess mos peoples
gonna lose.

—JOHN BERRYMAN

The Nine of Pentacles Reversed represents the tornado that comes sweeping through Martha's garden, smashing it to smithereens.

In other words, loss. Could be financial, could be personal. Your own responsibility for this loss—and chance of avoiding it in future—is questionable here. Perhaps you've been a little reckless. Maybe you've overlooked something. Or because, sometimes, life is just like that. People deceive you, weather goes sour, companies go belly-up. If you see this card in the future, you should be prepared for anything from an investment going bust, to your best friend lying to you, to your dog knocking over an antique lamp your grandmother left you.

So double check your finances, don't leave your purse lying around, and move that lamp to a safer spot.

TEN OF PENTACLES

WHY EARN WHEN
YOU CAN INHERIT?

Now, we're talkin' serious money. And more than money. Here the vision of wealth is tightly entwined with concepts of family and permanence. This could mean getting a big, fat inheritance, marrying into the Kennedy clan, or buying your dream home. This money could have a huge impact on your sense of status and security—and only in a positive sense. If you've ever dreamed of being one of the beautiful people, this could be your chance.

If this card turns up in your past, do you still have it? Or did you lose it all? A lot of times, this card shows up in the Hopes and Dreams position, and why not? Jeeves, my martini, please!

TEN OF PENTACLES REVERSED

WHY INHERIT WHEN YOU CAN BE ROBBED BLIND?

Unfortunately, just as Ten of Pentacles ups the happiness from Nine of Pentacles, Reversed ups the misery. If this card turns up reversed, do not invest in the stock market for a while. Either your judgment or your luck is impaired, and you could lose big time. If you've been counting on an inheritance, you may lose it. If something does come through, put it in the bank—in the safest, dullest account you can find.

This can also indicate a robbery or some sort of external hazard. Make sure you lock the door securely before going out. I know the neurotics among us don't like to hear this. You want to hear that you will be safe, and that the world is danger-free, even if you don't believe it. This time, I'm afraid, you're right to worry.

PAGE OF PENTACLES

A SOLID INVESTMENT.

Like all his fellow pages, the Page of Pentacles represents a young lad (or lass) just starting out. Either in grad school, or barely out of his student days, he's a serious, earnest guy. The Page of Pentacles has his head on straighter than some of his more flaky cohorts. Sure, he believes in doing good but, chances are, he'd rather write checks than start a community garden. Not that he's a Wall Street bully boy in the making. Rather he's the kind of guy who has a good job, a decent portfolio, and bought his house a long time ago when the rest of us were just renting. Whatever he does, he does thoroughly and well.

This card can also represent news, or a message of some kind. Remember, in plays, it's always the pages who rush onto the stage, yelling, "News from France, my lord!"

PAGE OF PENTACLES REVERSED

MONEY (AND TIME) DOWN THE TOILET.

Okay, if Pentacles Right Side Up is a clear-eyed young man with his future before him, Reversed is his goofy brother who plays in a bar band and borrows money from you. He's cute, he's funny, even if you don't always understand what he's saying. His beverage of choice is Bud—unless you're paying, in which case, it's a Stoli.

Unrealistic, he imagines himself a big fat rebel but, really, he just doesn't want to grow up. We have *all* dated people like this. If you are currently in such a relationship, he's not going to mature any time in the near future. If you're sick of hearing "I Fought the Law and the Law Won" and putting him to bed—dump him.

Not surprisingly, this card also represents Bad News. So, if you're not dating loser boy, you can expect disappointment in some area of your life anyway. Lucky you!

KNIGHT OF PENTACLES

YOUR MOM'S DREAM—AND
YOUR NIGHTMARE.

Oh, this is exactly the guy your mother wants you to marry. He's so responsible, so steady, so mature. So *boring!!*

No, really, he is a bit boring, the Knight of Pentacles. A solid, hard worker, he'll probably never cheat on you, and he'll always come through for you—unless, of course, you ask for excitement and spontaneity.

And he doesn't take a hint. When you say, You know what, next week is just a really busy time for me, he says, Okay, how about the week after? Part of his success in business is his persistence. And he's organized, and kind to animals and . . .

BORING!

KNIGHT OF PENTACLES REVERSED

JUST WHEN YOU THOUGHT IT COULDN'T GET WORSE....

Here we have our stolid old Knight of Pentacles, but he's not even responsible or hard working. This guy's just a narrow-minded bigot. He's very happy to tell you how this group or that group is ruining the country, but he'd never get his fat ass off the couch to do anything constructive. Like get a job.

Sure, he talks big, but he never seems to do anything about his grand schemes. We all have Knights of Pentacles Reversed somewhere in our family, Uncle So-and-So who can ruin a July Fourth faster than you can say "Haven't you had enough to drink?" Archie Bunker without the energy and sense of humor. I imagine sometimes he can be lovable. Sometimes you feel sorry for him. But most of the time you want to wring his neck.

QUEEN OF PENTACLES

"With great power there must also come great responsibility."

—SPIDER-MAN

Who wouldn't want to be the Queen of Pentacles? First of all, she's stinking rich. Doesn't have to worry about a thing, financially. Intelligent, talented, a woman of impeccable taste—think Jackie O. or Audrey Hepburn, that's the kind of charisma and quality we're talking about.

And—this is the really amazing part—she's generous. No Leona Helmsley she, she's intimately tuned in to the world around her and she uses her largesse to solve its problems. And she doesn't just write checks, she serves on boards, travels the world, speaks out when she has to. Now it's easy to say, Yeah, sure, if I had all that money, I'd be generous, too. Well, let's hope you do someday and let's hope you are.

QUEEN OF PENTACLES REVERSED

IT'S MINE! IT'S MINE, IT'S MINE, IT'S MINE!

If you think that the Queen of Pentacles Reversed must be poor, you haven't understood the true significance of the Queen of Pentacles. What's extraordinary about the Q of P is her sense of self-worth, a security that helps her help others.

Q of P Reversed may have just as much money as her philanthropist cousin, but she has none of her good points. She's terribly insecure, fake, phony, a big fat social climber. This is a woman profoundly ill at ease in the world. To cover that up, she'll find fault with everything you do, because she thinks it'll keep you from noticing how deeply screwed up she is. She's a nitpicker, this one. I hope you don't work for her. If you do, and you can't immediately get out of her orbit, try to put her at her ease as much as possible. You'll probably threaten her no matter what you do, because she's easily threatened, so keep your resume updated. But if you can prove to her you're not out to get her, you'll have a much easier time dealing with her.

Obviously, she can also be your mom, your sister, even your friend if you have poor judgment in human nature. As always, do a personal inventory. Have you been feeling crabby and mean-spirited lately? Indulged in a lot of bitchy comments about your friends? What's bugging you so badly that you feel the need to be such a moo?

KING OF PENTACLES

GOOD STEWARDSHIP.

In these days of corporate scandal, there are few people I can compare to the King of Pentacles—a businessman who is shrewd, successful, and above reproach. He has enormous power, but he uses it wisely. He doesn't even cheat on his wife.

For some women, this will no doubt represent the ideal man. For others, it may be the boss, or her father. Then again, for many, it may represent qualities she herself has or aspires to. Someone who has a sound material grasp of the world, and easily acquires wealth. Or, perhaps, a professor of math and science.

If you see this card in the future, it might indicate someone of this nature will have an impact on your life. Or it may indicate that you yourself will be entering a time when your financial acumen is extremely strong. Invest. Buy property. Apply for that high-powered Wall Street job. Now's your time.

KING OF PENTACLES REVERSED

IRRESPONSIBLE BASTARD.

Ah, here we have the Enron debacle. This king much resembles the first—except he has no moral restraints whatsoever. He, or she, will ruin anybody in order to get what he wants, throw people out of jobs to boost the stock price, and move the whole factory to some impoverished country and pay people two cents an hour.

He's as vulgar as Donald Trump's toupee, as greedy and irresponsible as a drunk at the beer spigot. Nothing is enough for this guy, because it's all about getting more, more, MORE! Naturally, if you're dating him, don't trust him as far as you can throw him, and make sure you get a good deal on the pre-nup. You'll be replaced by trophy wife number three in a heartbeat.

Again, if this is you, take a long, hard look at yourself. Where are your values? Do you have a life? Anyone you'd call a real friend? Somewhere along the career path, you took a wrong turn.

Wands

*W*ands are the most elusive suit in the deck. They represent the life force without the aggression of Swords, the monetary aspect of Pentacles, or the domesticity of Cups. In some decks they're called Clubs, but I think Wands is more apt, as it reflects their creativity and intellectual power. This force is the most cunning and the most adaptable of the four. It lives to fight another day.

ONE OF WANDS

IN THE BEGINNING....

You know the painting where God extends His finger to give Adam life? That finger is the One of Wands. It is *creation* with the full show of lightning bolts and hallelujahs. Birth of a child is not excluded here, but this is also the beginning of a new sculpture, a new business enterprise, anything that engages your intellect and emotions. It indicates great worldly success for your new venture. Thomas Edison probably got this card all the time, right before he invented the light bulb and a million other things. So stop screwing around with the cards and get moving!

ONE OF WANDS REVERSED

The best laid plans of mice and men
oft go aglay.

—ROBERT BURNS

It was all there, the great idea, the passion, the cosmic Ah-ha! And, yet, somehow, all that energy and brilliance just . . . petered out, came to nothing.

What went wrong? One day you were getting ready to climb Everest—the next, you were tossing all that very expensive climbing gear sitting in the back of your closet. The One of Wands Reversed indicates that the problem is—as it so often is—human. The other people you may have been working with screwed it up with their bickering. Or, you didn't have the most focused vision of your plans to start with. Or, you procrastinated and missed your shot.

But, the good news is, if you screwed it up, you have the power to fix it. Rise from the ruins of your false start and begin again.

TWO OF WANDS

THE SWEET AND SOUR
SMELL OF SUCCESS.

This is a complicated card and any attempt to simplify it makes it boring. The traditional image is of a lord looking out over his vast domain, while holding a globe in the palm of his hand. You have the impression of both enormous wealth and dissatisfaction. Some interpretations focus only on the wealth, seeing a powerful, dominant figure in charge of his/her world, a creative endeavor that will come to a good end, a career path that leads to good things.

The other side of this card is illness, sorrow—I'll stretch and call it depression. And that's where the globe comes in. It creates an image of someone who has a great deal, and yet fixates on what's left unconquered. You can see this card in at least two ways: success, and a reminder that success can't protect you from everyday troubles, such as illness or loss. Or, it suggests a success that feels less than perfect because no matter how successful you are, you're always going to feel dissatisfied and unworthy somehow. You decide which.

TWO OF WANDS REVERSED

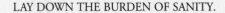

LAY DOWN THE BURDEN OF SANITY.

Well, if Right Side Up is complicated, Reversed is going to be complex as well. One interpretation is plain old unhappiness. Troubles, fear, heartache, toothache.

But another interpretation is a sense of wonder and enchantment—a direct contradiction of the depression and world-weariness of the Two of Wands. This is an appealing vision because it suggests that, sometimes, the best thing to do when you think you have it all and it still ain't enough is to let go. Find somewhere or something where you don't have all the power, where you can still be surprised. Lack of control makes most of us uncomfortable. But total control is impossible and, frankly, lonely.

So if you're feeling burned out, go to a movie. Take a walk in the woods. Let someone amaze you for a change.

THREE OF WANDS

MANY HANDS MAKE
LIGHT WORK.

This is an excellent card to find in the future of anyone starting a new job or business venture. In its most basic meaning, it represents trade, financial smarts, strength in negotiation. But some interpret this card as a link between partnership and prosperity. Often, the hardest part of success is getting someone to work with you, be it a colleague, or a bank, or contacts. This card indicates that you'll have no trouble finding those all-important connections and making them work for you.

If you see this card in the past, it might show that your current career or business situation started off with good support. Has that support dwindled? Why? Or, it might represent the model you work with best. Not everyone was meant to work with others. But if you do your best work in collaboration, maybe you should focus on finding the right people to work with.

THREE OF WANDS REVERSED

TOO MANY COOKS SPOIL THE BROTH.

Here we see the same theme of multiple efforts in a single venture but, upside down, the card reflects the negative aspects of that situation. People offering help that's not very helpful. Or, their motives are suspect. Or, it could indicate that you're not focused, rushing at a problem from all different directions, and not sure what to do or where to go next.

Notably, Arthur Edward Waite sees Three of Wands Reversed as a cessation of opposition. The roadblocks disappear, troubles melt away. Unfortunately, if the card is in the future, this either/or scenario isn't very illuminating. Are the people around you useful or not? It's safe to say, be wary.

FOUR OF WANDS

HOME IS WHERE THE HEART IS.

When your girlfriend who's getting married asks you to do a reading, this is absolutely the card you want to see at the end. The Four of Wands always reminds me of a Sukkoth tent, an image of prosperity and celebration after the labor of the harvest. It's a strong, rich image of domestic life.

Some books interpret this card a little more broadly to reflect the joy and material rewards that derive from any job well done. And this makes sense. There's something communal about the card that makes me think of family, but family is not necessarily husband, wife, and 2.5 kids. It could just as easily represent the full, busy life of a single person with a lovely home she's worked hard to build and which serves as a haven for her many, many friends—and maybe a few lovers.

Whatever your particular vision of heaven is, this happiness has been well earned.

FOUR OF WANDS REVERSED.

YOU'RE HAPPY—YOU JUST DON'T KNOW IT.

Most of the time, the Four of Wands doesn't really have a downside. Reversed, it means much the same as right side up: domestic bliss with a healthy side order of financial security. Not only is your home filled with love and laughter—it's going to be nicely decorated.

There are shades of doubt: a lack of security, inner turmoil, a yearning for a happiness. But such a strong card implies the roots of . . . oh, inner peace and tranquility, whatever you want to call it. They may need to be recognized, they may need you to nourish them. But you have what you need to make yourself happy. Spend a little less time obsessing about external success, the things other people have that you don't. Take a good look at what you do have. You might find it's more than enough.

FIVE OF WANDS

THE BOXING RING OF LIFE.

I always think of this as the Wall Street card. The traditional image is of five young men batting away at each other with poles. But you could update that to the hurly-burly of the trading floor: the ruthless drive for riches and success. Dangerous, high-stakes stuff.

If you see this card, you're either emerging from or entering a time of intense competition. What you want, others want, too. How hard are you willing to hustle? Some readers will no doubt take this as a metaphor for the dating scene, but, frankly, I think any arena that makes you work this hard for love and intimacy is not a good place to find intimate happiness. Interpretations vary slightly on the likelihood of success, but none of them say, Triumph after Much Tribulation. The card focuses on the fight, so get your boxing gloves on.

FIVE OF WANDS REVERSED

STABBED IN THE BACK.

Say what you will about the Five of Wands—it's straightforward, a fair fight. If you find the Five of Wands Reversed in the future, be very careful in whom you trust. Take nothing for granted. This is the card of legalese, doublespeak, backstabbing. Whatever endeavor you're about to embark upon—new job, house-buying—expect delays, indecision, frustration galore.

The only thing you can do is make sure that you yourself do not contribute to this mess. Be as clear and as well informed as you can. This is a card of Involvement, and while sometimes it may feel more liked Trapped, it's clear that you can't leave everything up to other people. That will only make it worse.

SIX OF WANDS

TO THE VICTOR GO THE SPOILS.

Congratulations, you've won. Or you're about to win.

The Six of Wands is about success, advancement, conquest. You were one of the five youths competing in the Five of Wands and you knocked everyone out. It hints at the labor that went into achieving this goal, but it symbolizes the moment when the gates open wide and you march through as the undisputed champ.

It's the phone call that says, "You got the job (or publishing contract or gallery show)." It's the meeting with your boss where she shuts the door and says, "We're promoting you." It's the moment when your lover says, "You know what? You're right and I'm wrong. Let's do it your way."

The nice thing about Wands is that, unlike Swords, there's very little aggression involved. It's more assertion. So, when you win, you don't leave people pissed off and humiliated. Enjoy your marbles.

SIX OF WANDS REVERSED

BARBARIANS AT THE GATE.

The traditional interpretation of the Six of Wands a man on horse-back, riding through the open gates of a conquered town. In the Six of Wands Reversed we can see that image in several negative lights, most of them relating to a sense of threat.

The first is your own fear. Hesitation. You know what to do, who to talk to, what to say, but you just don't have the guts to follow up.

The second is also fear, but this time you're standing on the other side of the gate, and someone's battering the door down. This is a siege situation. You're on the defensive. There is a sense of betrayal; someone's handed you over to the enemy. The card does not predict the outcome of the battle.

The third is possibly the toughest to handle: victory for someone else. The job or promotion went to another person, possibly your rival. Your sister just got engaged and everyone asks you the inevitable, hateful question, "So, when are *you* walking down the aisle?" Most of the time, when other people win, you don't lose—despite how it may feel. But this time, it does have some impact on your life. All you can do is grin and bear it.

SEVEN OF WANDS

CUE ROCKY THEME. . . .

This card combines the previous two: it indicates fierce competition and the necessity for combat, but also the strength to win, and the all-important upper hand. If you see this card in the present, know that you are in a serious fight. People either want the same thing you do, or want to stop you from getting it. Don't let the notion of conflict scare you off. You can win if you stay strong.

With Wands, I generally think of areas beyond the home: financial or career matters. You can easily interpret this card as pertaining to any office—a breeding ground of competition and malice. But, it could also indicate a legal matter, such as a quarrel with your land-lord. It could also refer to a creative or personal endeavor. Are you trying to set aside time and energy for one? Don't be so sensitive to everyone else's demands. Are you trying to sell a project? Get your name out there. Don't let your fear of rejection stop you.

This card might also apply to domestic situations. Do you feel you're the only one in your family operating in the realm of reality? Are there finances no one wants to sort out, a relative no one wants to help? Are you fighting with your whole family, trying to get them to face facts? If so, don't back down. You're the one in the right.

SEVEN OF WANDS REVERSED

PEACE IN OUR TIME.

So promised Neville Chamberlain, because everyone wanted peace—except Hitler, who, having gotten Czechoslovakia, went on to try and grab the rest of Europe.

The reversed position of this card reflects the things that keep us from fighting for what we know to be right. Namely, we chicken out. Interestingly, the card defines fear in a very petty, personal way. It's not fear that your opponent is going to whack you on the head. It's anxiety. Embarrassment, that little voice inside your head that says, "You're being such a *bitch!* Stop before everyone hates you."

This card warns against hesitation as well. Calm, rational assessment—yes. Dithering—no. She who hesitates, loses.

So, if you see this card in the future, beware that you're about to experience a failure of nerve. It may feel very sane and grown up: "Now, now, there's no need to fight." But, take the urge to pull back with a big grain of salt. Do you truly think you're going about getting what you want the wrong way—or do you just think it would be easier to stop fighting? So many times, we could avoid a lot of headaches and yelling by standing up for ourselves just once. But, instead, we back down even though we know we're right, and the problems just continue. So, make "peace" at your own peril.

EIGHT OF WANDS

BULLSEYE.

Here, for Wands, let's substitute arrows. An arrow flying through the air—*zing!*—straight into the target.

This card represents action and speed. Think of the sudden acceleration when a runner sprints toward the finish line. Whatever your goal is, events will proceed very quickly as you get closer to it. There's an element of hope here, the excitement of knowing that you're finally going to get what you want.

Are you moving too fast? Perhaps. So, as you speed along, just keep an eye out for Danger! Sudden Curve signs.

Now, for you romantics out there who are thinking, "Arrows? What about *Cupid*???"—you're right. This card also indicates love, the *coup de foudre*, the Glance Across a Crowded Room That Seals Your Fate.

EIGHT OF WANDS REVERSED

SPLAT.

Moving swiftly and steadily toward a goal . . . good. Speeding like a maniac, ignoring warning signs along the way . . . bad. The first of these is the Eight of Wands Right Side Up, the second is Eight of Wands Reversed.

There are downsides to speed. One is jumping to conclusions. This can lead to arguments, so no surprise that the Eight of Wands Reversed reflects dispute and discord. Jealousy also factors in here. That little stab of envy you get when your friend takes off all that weight and you've gained three pounds—it feels like an arrow to the heart, doesn't it?

Or, if you're not stabbed by envy, perhaps your conscience is stinging a little. Trample anyone on your dash up the ladder?

And, sadly, lovers, this card shows bad news for you, too. Fights, spats, domestic discord. Who knows? Maybe you took things a little too fast. . . .

NINE OF WANDS

TRAINING DAY.

Eating a lot of raw egg recently? That's not surprising. The Nine of Wands represents a state of preparedness with a hint of red alert. You either know or sense that opposition is about to rear its ugly head, and you're getting ready to stand your ground. What's the battle? Could be anything. Job, family, relationship. Look to the other cards or the subject of your reading to give you a clue.

This card also represents the calm before the storm, that sense of pause that often comes prior to the big blow-up; like in movies, when two armies meet on the battlefield, and they all just stand there glaring at one another before someone yells, *Charge!* And it's entirely possible that no one will yell Charge, that everyone will give up and go home. Just because you're ready for a fight doesn't mean the other person is. They may surrender before you even lift your sword. You look that mean.

Or, forget anticipation. It can also be just a boring old delay. Though ready for some action, you may have to wait a while. In the meantime, keep lifting weights.

NINE OF WANDS REVERSED

WEAK, WEAK, WEAK.

You skip a few raw eggs, go for the ice cream instead—and look what happens. The challenge comes, and you're not ready.

Nine of Wands Reversed represents adversity. Also calamity, which is adversity you weren't prepared for, and so you got royally screwed. It can also reflect a failure of nerve.

As opposed to the hearty fellow who usually appears on the Nine of Wands, here we have a vision of weakness, hardship, and ill health. So, all in all, if you see this card in the future, you know you'll face a lot of headaches and/or you aren't going to be at your strongest. It could be nothing more than a bout of flu when a crisis at work requires your attention. Or, it could be a wimpish moment when you pass up a chance to talk to your sister seriously about her borderline-abusive boyfriend.

See it in your past and it may explain some ongoing situations that frustrate you. Maybe when you feel stronger, you should deal with them.

TEN OF WANDS

WEIGHT OF THE WORLD.

Pressure, oppression, and heavy, heavy burden. This card feels familiar to women who take everything on their shoulders, whether it belongs there or not. The burden itself can involve many things: depression, overwork, a sense of feeling overwhelmed. The big question here is . . . is it all worth it? Are you working hard toward a successful conclusion? Or are you just floundering?

Some interpretations stress the element of disaster. The ruination of your plans has made you frazzled and distracted. Others emphasize striving toward a goal; you may be exhausted now, but it will all be worthwhile in the end. The key is to look at the other cards in the reading. What follows this card? If it's bad news, then you have some idea of what you're facing. If it's good news, then you can just about see the light at the end of the tunnel.

TEN OF WANDS REVERSED

PEOPLE PROBLEMS.

While the nature and outcome of the burden is uncertain in the Ten of Wands, the implication of Ten of Wands Reversed is squarely negative. If you get the Ten of Wands Reversed in a Present, Recent Past, or Future position, know that someone in your life is likely to cause you problems. If you're working with others toward a goal, you may discover that one of you is, well, a powerful-mad asshole: someone who secretly believes that it's all about them, and screw the rest of you.

Or, you're dealing with a plain old straightforward liar. Don't tell me: you recently hired a contractor, didn't you? If not, look around for a face card to see who the liar in your midst might be. Most likely, it's someone in your professional, as opposed to romantic, realm. However, if you and your partner are trying to resolve an issue, it may indicate that they're being less than open and cooperative. This person may even be perfectly nice in most respects. But they don't play well with others, and you could end up with sand thrown in your eyes.

PAGE OF WANDS

GOOD NEWS.

What do the sexy guy sitting alone at the bar and the postman have in common? They both present the titillating possibility of good news.

And that's the Page of Wands in a nutshell. A favorable shift in the winds, the arrival of someone with good intentions, a force there to help you. This is a trustworthy person, a loyal person. If a potential love interest, he won't cat around on you. If a new employee, she's not going to backstab you in the bathroom.

In an interesting side note, Waite informs us that if you see this card next to the Page of Cups, it indicates rivalry. Two beaux dueling for your hand? Make a nice change, wouldn't it?

PAGE OF WANDS REVERSED

BAD NEWS.

Run, don't walk, away from the guy at the bar. Ignore the flashing light on your answering machine—you don't need another melodramatic message from your crazy brother, claiming that dad is *torturing* him and, by the way, can he borrow a hundred bucks?

All the wonderful steadfast loyalty in this card is turned upside down. Instead, you have bad news, nasty comments, and bitchy gossip. Someone is stirring the pot and, not surprisingly, no one's getting along very well. The person represented in this card may have a lot of superficial charm, but he's essentially a narcissistic troublemaker. Most books warn that if this card reflects a love interest, the love's all on your side. He or she will break your heart. Avoid, avoid, avoid.

KNIGHT OF WANDS

GERONIMO!

You either have, or will soon take, a flying leap into the future. The flight into the unknown is now boarding at Gate 23.

The Knight of Wands moves fast. He doesn't like to stay in one place very long. He's about departures, changing places, absence. If you see him in a crucial spot in your reading, he can represent anything from moving to a new home, or a switch in jobs, to starting over in a whole new town.

The ultimate nature of the change is not indicated here. Are you going to be happy? Miserable? It doesn't say. But I'm generally in favor of change, so I say, go for it.

KNIGHT OF WANDS REVERSED

SHIT HAPPENS.

When the Knight of Wands is reversed, the nature of the break in your routine becomes clearer: it sucks. Well, maybe not sucks, but it isn't easy. This change takes you by surprise, disrupts your life, makes you question some of your most significant relationships. This could all be for the good, of course, but it's not a whole lot of fun while you're going through it.

Rupture, interruption, confusion—it's all here. This card indicates quarreling, also romantic jealousy and discord. One of the least fun things about crisis is the way certain people fall apart, leaving you to handle all the shitwork. The only thing I can recommend with this card is, try and see the long view. And if that doesn't work, drink.

THE QUEEN OF WANDS

SALT OF THE EARTH.

The Queen of Wands is the ideal friend. She's warm, understanding, nonjudgmental, and has a great, earthy sense of humor. She's never jealous or grasping, because she's completely secure within herself and her domain. Don't mistake her for a pushover, however; she is, after all, a queen and queens have power.

But mostly she has a sympathetic ear and gives solid, practical advice. For all her love of nature and devotion to the home, she also has an aspect of money or business success. She's a very good person to go to for career help or a fresh take on your financial problems. If she turns up in your reading, it may be a sign that you need outside advice on your issue. Consult a shrink, a money manager, or your most mature friend. The Queen of Wands may not be the flashiest, most exciting person in the tarot deck but, let's face it, the world would be a much better place if there were more people like her.

THE QUEEN OF WANDS REVERSED

✦

GREEN-EYED MONSTER.

Experts hold conflicting visions of the Queen of Wands Reversed, but they all agree on one aspect: jealousy.

The strong sense of self that makes the Queen of Wands so generous to others disappears when the card's upside down. This woman is envious, unstable, and ready to turn on you in a heartbeat. She'll whack you in the head with her wand, then tell you it was for your own good.

Because she is a Queen, she probably holds some position of authority. This is not good. If she's your boss, definitely take her criticism with a grain of salt (and get your resume in order if it looks like she's not going anywhere). Some poor ladies may see their mother in this card; if so, get thee to a shrinkery and try to . . . detach, as they say. You might also ask yourself, do you have a friend who's always telling you what you're doing wrong with your life? That your boyfriend doesn't treat you well enough, that your workplace is screwing you over, and that, by the way, you could really stand to lose a few pounds? Do you feel strangely like shit every time you see her? Next time, before you start nodding your head in agreement, ask yourself just *why* she feels so compelled to put you down. What's wrong with *her* life?

KING OF WANDS

RULER OF HIS DOMAIN.

All kings have their domain. Cups has the spiritual, creative realm; Pentacles is your money man; and Swords is the ultimate judge.

At first glance, the King of Wands seems to be lacking a kingdom. Like his spouse, the Queen, he is a happy, generous fellow, closely tied to his home and the world of nature. He's described as married, fatherly. He's a good, steady friend. Above all, he's honest. If he says he will do something, he does it. Waite says, somewhat elliptically, that the card may indicate news relating to family or inheritance.

Who is he? Well, if you recognize him already, then that person will be integral to the issue you are dealing with. If not, he may be a future boss, a teacher, possibly a love interest. Sometimes, if I see him in the future in a question about a troubled relationship, I anticipate that things will soon improve.

But I think the ultimate point about the King of Wands is that he is master of his own soul. He represents integrity, unspoiled and unconcerned by the demands of the outside world. I could add some blah blah about that being the most important realm of all, but I think you get the picture.

KING OF WANDS REVERSED

THINKS HE'S RULER OF YOUR DOMAIN. . . .

Well, you know those hardcore, self-sufficient types. They can get a little full of themselves. A little closed-minded. And we see that with the King of Wands Reversed.

The King of Wands Reversed is still a good guy, but you can use the word "severe" to describe him. Because he's pulled himself up by his bootstraps, he feels everyone should do likewise. Dogmatic, he has a slightly inflated sense of himself and, as a result, gets into arguments much more often than our friendly, open-minded King of Wands.

This could represent many people in your life. You either recognize him or you don't. But the two kings represent an interesting split in how you can view your own happiness and success. Happiness can be a reason to share with others . . . or an opportunity to judge others.

Swords

Swords are, as you might expect, all about power. Power is tricky for some women. We want it, we like it. Yet, we want everyone to like us, and fear that they won't if we assert ourselves.

But Swords are not about self-restraint, they're about power. And that means influencing, affecting and, yes, sometimes bothering, other people. There's nothing wrong with this. The only issue that remains is: How do you use your power? For good or ill?

ONE OF SWORDS

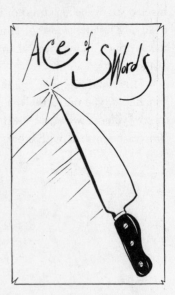

VICTORY!

Like all Aces, this one represents the beginning of something. It's activity, aggression . . . conquest. So, what have you been wanting to conquer lately? Whether it's your career, or the inevitable guy, you're in the right frame of mind. You're ready to go and the results should be successful. Now, there's something slightly excessive about this card. Powerful people tend to go their own way; they do listen to others, but not a lot. If they love or hate, it's to an intense degree. Take care. Don't start out at a level you can't maintain. Balance! You don't want to change from warrior to worrier midstream.

ONE OF SWORDS REVERSED

BOSSY BOOTS.

If you see this card reversed, that indicates that whatever venture you've embarked upon will not turn out as you hoped. Severity ranges from disappointment to debacle.

What happened?

The good news is that the answer lies with you, so if this card appears in the future, you still have time to change your approach. Right now, you're on track to piss a lot of people off. Power is one thing. Bullying is another. As you stomp all around in your big boots, the troops are starting to feel rebellious.

So what, says you. I'm goddamn ATTILA THE HUN! Screw them.

But that approach only works so long—usually right up until the point where your staff quits en masse, your friends stop talking to you, and your boyfriend withholds sex, because—you know what? Attila the Hun just doesn't turn him on. Powerful women, absolutely. But Hilda, Mistress of Pain, he'll skip.

Lighten up! No woman is an island. Even Patton had to buy the troops a round once in a while.

TWO OF SWORDS

STEEL AGAINST STEEL.

Just like in the movies, two swords come crashing down. In the center, they meet, and go *klang!* For a moment, they're motionless, perfectly matched in tension, and you're wondering, Okay, when's Errol Flynn going to wheel around and cut the other guy's head off?

Not in this card. This card is about the *klang!* The stillness. The balance. The . . . stalemate? Well, possibly. Generally, balance indicates a kind of harmony, but we are talking about swords here. Weaponry usually suggests aggression or action of some kind. Is this a meeting of the minds or the start of a fight? A state of equality or opposing forces canceling each other out?

Well, it depends on what the other cards tell you. The Two of Swords has the feel of a truce, a state of balance and harmony between opposing forces. Agreement—even conformity. But perfect balance can also mean inertia. You have to stay still to stay upright. So, I look at this card and see a moment of expectation, which can also mean waiting. You want something, you have reason to believe it will come through, but not quite yet. If you see this card in any of the three future positions, it indicates a possible pause in the proceedings. If you're hoping for a promotion or a proposal, you might have to wait a bit longer than you thought. Be patient.

TWO OF SWORDS REVERSED

EVASION.

Now here we see some action—maybe. This can indicate a point of release, movement in your life affairs. But not necessarily. The strongest aspect of this card is duplicity.

There's something honest and forthright about two burly men coming together and swapping saber-sparks. They're laying it out on the table, right here, right now. But Two of Swords Reversed suggests that whatever struggle you're engaged in now, you're operating without all the facts. Either someone hasn't told you the whole truth and nothing but the truth—or you're not being honest with yourself.

So, if you feel like you're thrashing around in a swamp and getting nowhere, hold still a minute. Where are you headed? Who's directing you? How good is their eyesight and how invested are they in seeing you make progress? Not all that much? Maybe that's why you're stuck.

THREE OF SWORDS

STORMY WEATHER.

Notice how all the bad news romance clichés involve threes. "Three's a crowd." Romantic "triangle." There's a general acknowledgment that, other than the Holy Trinity and the Bee Gees, three is a problematic number.

So, not surprisingly, the Three of Swords is a bummer card for anyone doing a relationship reading, unless it comes in a Present or Recent Past position, in which case, they already knew. It indicates separation, whether fighting, physical distance, or that cow he insists is just a drinking buddy. The traditional image for this card is a heart, pierced by three swords. Get the picture?

THREE OF SWORDS REVERSED

CLOUDY VISION.

The Three of Swords Reversed also indicates romantic difficulties, but to a much less intense degree. Instead of screaming, you're snapping. You don't feel hatred, but mistrust. You haven't found the frilly underwear in his car—but you have your suspicions.

Actually, you're not sure what to think, and that's one of your problems. Three of Swords Reversed is a nightmare card for anyone prone to second-guessing herself. You know you can talk yourself into believing the worst about anything and anybody. What you don't know is what to do! You're obsessing and confused. This card reminds me of how people act when they hear rumors of layoffs in a company. Everyone's gathering in offices, fretting over the latest bit of gossip, and no one really knows anything, but talking about what they think they know makes them feel better.

Only worrying doesn't really help, does it? In the end, it's better to detach, to wait and see. If the other shoe exists, it will drop when it's ready.

FOUR OF SWORDS

TIME OUT.

The traditional image for this card is a knight lying on a coffin. And yes, he looks quite dead. But, fear not, this is not a Death card.

We might call this card Burn Out. Which, as we all know, can feel a lot like death. You've been so intensely involved with life—for good, or ill, or both—your mind and body are not functioning properly anymore. It's not time to cut back or slow down. It's time to stop. Do nothing, lie on a beach, watch gobs of TV, take long walks through the woods. Whatever you need to do.

If you see this card in the present, it's probably not a big surprise. You know you're fried. If you see it in the future, know that life will soon get so crazy you will need to take some time off. And when that time comes, recognize it, and don't beat yourself up. (See Sample Reading Number One. The Four of Swords figures prominently.)

In a slight variation, it could indicate, not so much a state of exhaustion, as a time of reassessment. If you're in the process of figuring out What Comes Next, you probably won't be as fully engaged as you have been in the past. You've taken a step back, retreated slightly. Some might accuse you of "not being there." But how else can you get a proper perspective, except from a distance?

FOUR OF SWORDS REVERSED

EASY DOES IT.

Rather than the frenetic activity that made you into a zombie, The Four of Swords Reversed suggests moderate action. Or tentative, unfocused action. Whatever the opposite of full-tilt boogie is, that's the Four of Swords Reversed.

Whether it's Future, Present, or Past, you're keeping your cards pretty close to the vest. This is either wise or paranoid. You're not taking huge risks—except for the risk of non-commitment. Should you be putting yourself forward more? That depends to some degree on what the other cards show you.

This card could also represent those first hesitant steps back into the hurly-burly after your period of rest and repose. In which case, caution is advisable. You can't go from 0 to 180 in five seconds. That's a good way to stall out, or worse—crash.

FIVE OF SWORDS

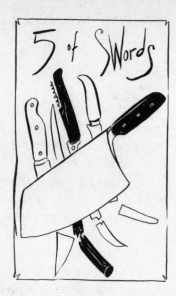

BLACK MONDAY.

It's a fact of life: sometimes you try . . . and fail.

And this time, you didn't just fail. Oh, no. This time, the good guys didn't just lose, the bad guys won. This is humiliation. Aggression. Conquest. And lots and lots of gloating.

The Five of Swords is an Ouch card. It's the party where your ex shows up with his new girlfriend—the beautiful, kind, thoughtful one everyone adores. It's the Big Mistake at the Office, the one that's all your fault, and will cost a million dollars to fix. Some days, you just have to eat shit.

If this card occurs in the future, it suggests one of two things: total disaster for you or victory for you, but at the expense of others. (Yep, it's possible that the aggressor in this scenario, the jerk waving the sword and pumping her fist . . . is you. In which case, I would suggest you stop it right now. You're creating a karmic nightmare.) But, if it's the former, and you're the one hurting, just remember that conquest and aggression used to mean rampaging Visigoths who disemboweled your nearest and dearest, and then raped your schnauzer for kicks. Compared to that, you probably got off easy.

FIVE OF SWORDS REVERSED

GRAY TUESDAY.

The Five of Swords Reversed also indicates loss or failure, but to a lesser degree. Rather than falling victim to an aggressive, nasty schmuck, you run afoul of a weak, forgetful person—either yourself or someone else—who doesn't look after your interests properly. Your dippy boss who might not push hard enough with her boss for the raise you deserve. Or your beau forgets your birthday—again—prompting you to seriously reconsider the future of this relationship.

And, of course, it could also be you. See this card in the future, and you should look out for those who are careless with the lives of others, and wary of your tendencies to be careless about your own life. Keep sharp.

SIX OF SWORDS

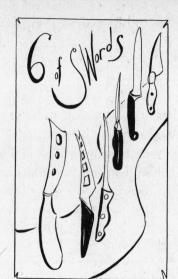

CROSSING THE RIVER.

If you've been having a rotten time of it—and I assume you have in some respect, because you're doing a reading—this card will come as a relief. You're about to make a journey. Yes, I know, that sounds like a hoary old fortune-teller but, no, really. This card indicates moving away from unhappiness. Could be mentally, as in a new frame of mind where everything doesn't look so bleak. Or, could be physically, as in leavin' on a jet plane. But the main point is, you're leaving a bad situation behind.

Now, change brings anxiety. You may worry: Am I being too hasty? Am I missing something? There's no guarantee of what's ahead. Some cards in the tarot deck will tell you yes, you are being hasty; slow down, reassess. But not the Six of Swords. Wherever you're going, it can't be as bad as where you've been!

SIX OF SWORDS REVERSED

LOW TIDE.

Interpretations differ on the meaning of Six of Swords Reversed. Some say that it simply shows a stalemate or an inability to move forward. For whatever reason, the journey is delayed—*not* canceled!—and, for now, you're stuck. We all know that state of mind: Agh, I'm so crazed, I don't know *what* to do. After spinning around in circles, you're too dizzy to take a step.

It could also indicate a proposal, sometimes of love. Yay! Prince Charming comes riding to the rescue. Some interpretations place the stress on the unwanted nature of the proposal; in other words, it's icky. Like when your boss takes a huge mess and puts it on your desk with a big fat smile that says, "Gotcha now." Or the icky guy in marketing asks you out.

What the two interpretations have in common is that you are not the active person here. If change comes, it's external. Perhaps the best thing to do is take a deep breath and realize sometimes the best way to get out of a hellish situation is to stop worrying about it. Let go. The tide always comes in sooner or later.

SEVEN OF SWORDS

PLANNING STAGES.

The Seven of Swords is one of the more complicated cards in the tarot deck. Even Arthur Edward Waite had trouble figuring it out. The traditional image is a man walking, hurrying off with five swords in his arms. Grinning, he looks over his shoulder to see two more, stuck in the ground behind him. Is he stealing the swords? Is he gathering them up, bringing them to the battlefield? Does the division of swords—some in his arms, some still in the ground—indicate conflicting impulses?

Here we see the early stages of a plan. That could be hope, dreaming, and first designs. Or, in a less positive light, it can be envy, or even an attempt to take what's not yours. This makes sense, as sometimes we don't know what we want until we see someone else who has it. Jealousy is annoying, but it does cut through denial.

There's a strong element of unreliability here. Again, any plan in the early stages is uncertain. How much of it is fantasy? How hard are you willing to work? How trustworthy are the other people involved?

All this is not to say that the plan—be it a new career path, an exercise regimen, a home ownership scheme—will fail. Just that it's very, very fragile right now. Don't mistake the first breathless fantasy for the dream fulfilled.

SEVEN OF SWORDS REVERSED

LET'S TALK.

The Reversed Position of this card represents that inevitable follow-up to a great idea: talking about it. This could mean advice—whether good advice or bad advice depends on the other cards. Since we don't quite know the quality of the original plan, we can't know the quality of the counsel. But you're discussing it with a friend, your accountant, your parents.

Or, it could also mean people are talking about you—and not always positively. "My God, she thinks she's going to start a catering business? Give me a break, she's still paying off her college loan!"

Or, it could mean that useless chatter that follows after you come up with a plan, the yak-yak about all the irrelevant details so you don't actually have to deal with the boring stuff. "Definitely, the logo should be pink, no question." "So, have you applied for a business loan yet?" "Nah, I'll think about that later!"

But I always interpret this card for myself this way: second-guessing. Self-doubt. That gloomy voice that moans, "You can't do this. This won't work out. This is a disaster. Don't even try! You'll get hurt! You'll be humiliated!"

In a word, neurosis.

So, what should you do with all this talk? Don't take it too terribly seriously. Listen to what feels solid and practical, be wary of the rest. Talk is the enemy of action.

EIGHT OF SWORDS

ALL TIED UP AND
NOWHERE TO GO.

The image for this card shows a woman tied up and blindfolded—
and not in that fun, kinky, Hey-honey-let's-try-something-new kind
of way. You're in a bad, bad situation without a clue how to get out of
it. This is a crisis, conflict, a miserable position to be in. The particu-
lars can run the gamut from abusive relationships to a stagnant, frustrating job. Anything that makes you feel depressed, belittled, and
exhausted—and from which you just can't pull yourself free.

If this card turns up in the past, it might indicate why you hesitate to take risks in the present. Having been badly burned, you
might not trust your ability to judge people and events. If it's in the
present, well, at least you know it's not all in your head. Someone or
something really is tormenting you. If it turns up in the future, and
you're thinking about a new venture, be it business or romantic, take
heed. Can you see any signs that your new boss or beau is, in fact, a
sadist? Are you deliberately ignoring the big flashing sign that says
DANGER? What do the other cards indicate about the duration of
this hog-tied state? Is it a temporary thing or the end result?

EIGHT OF SWORDS REVERSED

HIGH AND DRY LAND.

There are slight variations on the meaning of this card, but generally it reflects either a less intense version of the Eight of Swords, or the aftermath of the Eight of Swords. It's depression, anxiety, a sense of unease. Now, if you just got out of the mess reflected in the previous card, well, no wonder you feel a little uneasy. But you will have to move on if you don't want that evil force to control your life forever.

Another interpretation is hard work, which many people turn to as a way of recovering from a traumatic situation. Or, sometimes, work is *so* hard that it becomes oppressive and limiting. But some people see this card as hopeful, the point where you start to free yourself from a horrible entanglement. If you don't feel totally up to it yet, don't worry. Just act like you do. You'd be amazed how often that works.

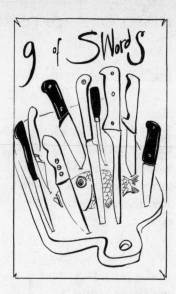

TEARS ON MY PILLOW.

Here we have another unhappy lady. This one has woken up in the middle of the night and is weeping. It generally means suffering, despair, and anxiety. Even—it must be said—illness and even death.

The card strongly suggests that another person is involved here. You may be worried about someone else, or troubled by a situation not of your own making. You might expect to see this card in a reading for someone whose parent is seriously ill, or whose husband has lost his job, or who is experiencing a crisis of trust.

This is not a happy card. Hopefully, it will turn up in the past. But if it turns up in the future, it's telling you that something unfortunate is going to happen, possibly to someone you care about, and it's going to demand your energy and attention. Perhaps the only advice I can give is that staying up till three in the morning worrying doesn't actually help anyone. Be there—but try not to fall apart.

NINE OF SWORDS REVERSED

DIRTY LITTLE SECRETS.

Here, the difficulties are more specific: suspicion, doubt, gossip. This card represents the damage people can do with their tongues, whether spreading false rumors or spilling the beans. I would expect to see it in a reading for someone who thinks their loved one is cheating on them or a colleague is doing them dirt in some way. Other elements of this card are fear and timidity. You know you should say something, confront them but, oh, my God, what happens then? So, you live in torment and uncertainty.

Are you right to be suspicious? Well, the term "reasonable fear" is often mentioned, so, sadly, your suspicions may be well-founded. The only way you'll know is to demand the truth.

One interpretation says that the Nine of Swords Reversed is the direct opposite of the Nine of Swords. In other words, healing, restored peace of mind, good news. You've made it through the wilderness and ended up safe and sound on the other side. If this card turns up in the future, you'll have to be very honest with yourself and decide which is the more likely outcome.

TEN OF SWORDS

PINNED TO THE MAT.

You can't mess around with the Ten of Swords, so I'll give it to you straight: It's disaster. Tears, misery, pain, ruin . . . a veritable cornucopia of bad news.

Hopefully, this card turns up either in the Past, or in your Hopes and Fears area. But if it is in the Future position, then you should prepare for the fact that you may be doing some crying at some point. The Ten of Swords doesn't generally mean romantic disaster. This is probably a reversal in the legal, global sense—a setback that affects your standing and security in the world.

Most importantly, it does not mean death. And, as long as you're not dead, you have the power to pick yourself back up (after you pull all those swords out of your ass) and move on.

TEN OF SWORDS REVERSED

GOOD THINGS IN SMALL PACKAGES.

Here we have small signs of improvement. A modest raise. A pat on the back. A contact for a great job. You may even win the lottery. It won't be enough money for you to retire on, but you can probably buy yourself something nice at Saks.

If you see this card in the future, and you've been having a rough time of it, know that the universe has begun to smile on you once more. (Or, at least, it's stopped crapping on your head.) Bear in mind, none of these things are final or permanent. They don't represent the total reversal of bad fortune you might have been hoping for, but enough to put a spring in your step again. It's not long-lasting, so take whatever emotional, material advantage you can from it and build on that.

Conversely, if you've been hoping for Big Things—that promotion, that ring, that career breakthrough—this card warns you that sometimes good things come in small packages because they are . . . small. You don't always take the Great Leap Forward. Sometimes it takes baby steps.

PAGE OF SWORDS

CONSULT THE ORACLE.

All the figure cards in the Suit of Swords represent various degrees of strength—ranging from intuition to brute force. The Page of Swords, being the low man on the totem pole, presents us with the least potent of these, which is . . . gossip. Okay, call it the ability to gather information. Find out what other people don't want you to know. Keeping your finger on the pulse.

Basically, this card shows you someone who always has their ear to the ground. Whatever the latest office scuttlebutt, they're going to know it first. They have insight into people's motives, pick up on vibes others miss, and they *always* know who's doing who.

So, what does this mean to you? Well, generally, the court cards represent a person influential in your current situation. In a present or future position, this card might suggest the need for information. There's more here than meets the eye—well, *your* eye anyway. To figure out what that is, you should consult someone who knows more than you do, or who can see things with a fresh perspective. That could be a good friend, the boss's assistant, or even a shrink. Whoever you talk to, they can reveal an essential piece of information.

PAGE OF SWORDS REVERSED

FIND THE WEAKEST LINK.

The Page of Swords Reversed offers various interpretations of help-lessness. Somewhere, you have a weak link in your chain. It could be an outside person who's let you down: your assistant, who has no clue what she's doing, makes you look bad; a friend, on whom you've relied, isn't such a good friend, after all.

It could also mean that illness is about to descend: a debilitating flu, a bout of back trouble. Or else you might soon find yourself in a crummy situation that you weren't prepared for and have no power to change. If the card comes up in your future, then you should sit back and wait to fight another day. You're in no position to argue with fate right now.

This is also an interesting card to show up in the seventh or eighth positions—the ones that reveal how you see yourself and how others see you. Often, we think we're weaker than we are in relation to others. So, if this card appears there, ask yourself if you couldn't be a little more assertive.

KNIGHT OF SWORDS

HERE I COME TO SAVE THE DAY!

This card embodies strength in the most Hollywood sense: bravery, derring-do. Russell Crowe with a touch of Mad Max. The person described here is not a wild-eyed killer; he's a little impetuous, heedless of the consequences maybe, but smart, with some degree of justice on his side. But he or she is reckless, and they have a lot to think about other than your best interests—although they do expect your full cooperation.

This card often represents an important event in your life. It happens very fast and then it's over, but it leaves a significant and lasting impact.

If your question was romantic in nature, it could reflect an affair that's full throttle, no looking back—all wonderfully dramatic and exciting. But be careful you don't spin out and crash. Or, maybe you're involved with a cop or a fireman.

Or, the card could represent your boss, determined to buck the corporate bully boys. You think she's just swell, but what happens if they fire her—and maybe you?

Whatever it is, bravo to them for being so brave and noble. But you, my dear, should proceed with caution—and stay away from the sword.

KNIGHT OF SWORDS REVERSED

MIGHTY MOUTH.

Here we have the downside of all of the above. A big fat pain in the ass—even if he or she is in the right, this person's manner is so bullying and obnoxious, it could hardly matter less. He's into power, although he'll probably insist it's all for the public good.

In a less personal sense, this card reflects poor judgment, bad impulse control, a lack of self-restraint. So, if you get this card in the future, watch yourself. You'll be dealing with someone whose sense of what's appropriate or necessary is seriously off. Or, you could be a little out of control. This could be an ill-advised affair, an unnecessary fight, any bout of emotional self-indulgence.

But if the card strongly reminds you of someone you know, it would be a very good idea to put some distance between you and this individual. They sound like a major headache.

QUEEN OF SWORDS

OUR LADY OF SORROWS.

If you're look at this card and thinking, Cool, Xena, Warrior Princess!—think again. Remember that the chief interpreter of the tarot was a man who grew up in the reign of Queen Victoria. So, while many of us might see a woman with sword as a good thing, he saw a symbol of sterility. A woman who has experienced great sorrow and who has been made bitter by the trials of her life. It's an image of mourning, loss, the twilight of life.

Other interpreters have tried to soften this vision a bit, adding the qualities of intelligence, perception, and ability to command to the mix. But we have to face the fact that the Queen of Swords is not a happy lady. This card is generally seen as an older woman, and when trying to figure out who she is and what effect she has on your life, an obvious place to start would be your mom. Did she have a rough time of it? Did those difficulties make her a pissy, suspicious person? Most importantly, has she imparted that distrust to you? Or did you rebel, leaping heedlessly into everything, just to prove to her that the world can be trusted?

Other possibilities include a boss, a friend, or a sister. Whoever she is, she's affecting your life right now, either as an unacknowledged influence or a very much acknowledged pain in the ass.

QUEEN OF SWORDS REVERSED

BEE–YOTCH.

Let's be kind and grant that this Queen has also been through the wringer. However, the Queen of Swords Reversed hasn't turned her anger inward to punish herself, she's turned it on other people. This card represents malice, cruelty, spitefulness. This is definitely that disappointed person at the office who never has a good word to say about anyone. Or your neighbor, the one always peeking out her door to see if you're coming home with someone so she can bad-mouth you as a slut.

I also think this could represent an ungenerous social dynamic, a phase you're going through with a group of friends: bitchy, negative, supposedly supportive. But notice how when anyone tries to move on, everyone tears her down?

If you don't immediately recognize the person, think about where you're blocked. Might there be someone poisoning the well? Spreading nasty rumors about you? Somewhere in your life, there's a malign force. Call in the witch doctor.

KING OF SWORDS

HERE COMES THE JUDGE.

As anyone who's done jury duty knows, there are all kinds of judges. Benevolent judges, ball-busting judges, the ones who let you off with a slap on the wrist, and the ones who put you in jail for life.

You don't argue with the King of Swords. He is the one in control, he has all the power. And the sword is not a flashy accessory: he has sway over life and death. He is not unfair, but he's not deeply sympathetic either. This is a dispassionate judge.

If I see this card in a reading, I would guess that a time of judgment is coming up. It could be as obvious as your year's review at the office, or as broad as a time in your life when what you do will have significant repercussions in the present and future. Some times in our lives, our actions don't mean very much; we can go back, apologize the next day, all forgotten. This card indicates consequences. If you see this card in the future, you will probably be coming up against a powerful authority figure of some kind. Make sure you're ready.

KING OF SWORDS REVERSED

HANGING JUDGE.

Power corrupts. Absolute power . . . you know the rest. Here we see all the negative aspects of authority. Cruelty, insensitivity, someone who runs roughshod over others to attain his or her goals—or just to make himself or herself feel better. Put bluntly: A rotten little sadist.

The King of Swords is such a strong figure, you probably have a strong sense of who it is; he's not the kind of guy who goes unnoticed. But looking at it in a broader sense, you could be coming into a time—or hopefully just leaving one—when the universe just wasn't playing fair. Whatever you did, it either fell short or it was flat out wrong. There are times in life when we moan, "It's just not fair." And we're right.

Strange but True
Tales of Tarot Number Three

The Girl Who Got Her Wish

I once worked with a woman who had a thing for the boss. He was a little older than she was, not married, but she figured he'd never be interested in her, and so she was content to lust from afar. More or less.

But then she noticed he seemed to be going out of his way to spend time with her, and hope took wing. She got up the nerve to ask him to a party her friend was giving and, lo and behold, he showed up. (Late, but he showed up.) Afterwards, they walked home together and their love blossomed on the street corner.

She woke up the next morning, convinced she was in love. Told everyone: I have met *the* man, I am *in love*.

Okay, you know how this story ends, right? They dated for three weeks and then he dumped her.

Now, this guy wasn't a terrible guy. In fact, he was probably right to dump her. They had less than zilch in common, and whenever they were together, she was so busy being in awe of him, she never bothered to ask herself if she was actually having a good time.

But this was the first time she ever thought she was in love, so it was hard to let go.

Really hard.

And the fact that she had to see him every day at work didn't help.

Normally a fairly rational gal, my friend was in full-throated "If I don't get him back, my life will be ruined" mode.

Enter tarot cards . . .

All the time she's shuffling, she's muttering, Will we be together? Will we be together? Will we be together? Will we be together?

And would you believe it? The cards said *yes*?

There was all sorts of misunderstanding and mismatch in the early part of the reading. But the Future cards were all passion, sex, connection. (No home and hearth cards, I noticed, but it was early days.) Despite my doubts about the whole thing, I had to admit, the future looked pretty rosy for this sundered pair.

Optimism and confidence restored, my friend stopped avoiding the boss. Started joining the gang at those after-work drinking fests that are a part of every twenty-something's work life. One night, she was sitting next to the boss, and thought that she would subtly let him know of her continued interest by groping him under the table.

He groped her back.

They proceeded to her house for a bout of drunken, frenetic sex. . . .

And that was it.

That's all she got. A one-night stand. No whispered words of remorse, no I'll call you's, nothing. But, frankly, in the cold, hungover morning light, the supposed love of her life wasn't looking all that irreplaceable.

A few months later, he moved on to someone else. And a few months after that, my friend moved on to a new job.

No more sleeping with the boss.

Sample Readings

In order to give you some idea of the many and varied meanings of the cards in context, I'm going to describe some readings I did for friends and clients. Hopefully, they'll demonstrate how, in a tarot reading, it's more important to look at the overall story rather than any single card.

A few months ago, my husband and I, after years of apartment hunting in Brooklyn, decided to move to Queens. We found a big, gorgeous place, and made the switch from renters to homeowners for the first time in our lives. Great, right? Except that I had lived in Brooklyn since college, and Queens seemed like a million miles away from everything I found familiar and comfortable. And, if I didn't like it, I couldn't just move—not with a mortgage hanging over my head.

So, thinking hard on my new apartment and nabe, everything I liked and everything I didn't like, I asked the cards...

Will I be happy in Queens?

Here's what I got.

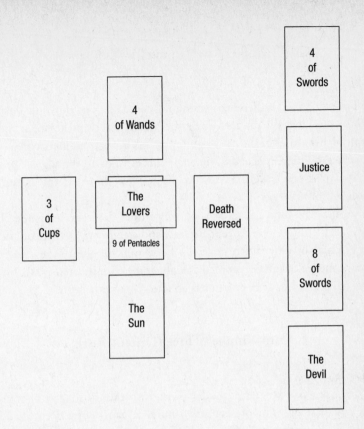

Card Number One (Present Position)

The Nine of Pentacles

The center card is essentially your situation and the core emotions surrounding it. For a question about home and hearth, the Nine of Pentacles is an apt card. It represents happiness in your own space, a nurturing attitude toward the home. A place for everything and everything in its place—including you.

As it happened, I had just started working out of the home, and was having a very fulfilling time of it. So, this card indicated a strong, positive attachment to the home, which was great, but would not be so great if my next home was uncongenial in any way.

Card Number Two (Immediate Influence)

The Lovers

The second card represents a strong influence on your situation. And while the Lovers is the card every sex-hungry gal wants to see at the end of her reading, the card also represents a balanced love, uncomplicated by hidden agendas, material concerns, or all those great unspoken "issues." Well, as uncomplicated by those things as any relationship ever gets.

Since this was a reading about my future domestic happiness, I was very pleased to see love, harmony, and stability right there on the horizon. Not only did it generally bode well for the future, but it made me feel whatever problems might come with the new place, my husband and I had the emotional bond to cope with them.

Card Number Three (Distant Past)

The Sun

I think of this card as the Freudian card. It reveals the shadow of your distant past on your present and future. It can be the deep, dark, buried thing that still tints your vision of life, or that wonderful childhood experience that forever defined your vision of happiness and security.

The Sun is a great card, a wonderful card. It symbolizes friends and good food and honorable happiness and great sex—everything you want in life. (In fact, I would much rather have this card turn up later in the reading, but hey. . . .)

In this case, I knew exactly what the Sun represented: the apartment I grew up in. It was a huge, old-fashioned New York apartment, the kind no one but millionaires can afford now. I had given up any hope of finding something like it. But, in fact, the apartment in Queens was very similar, a sort of peewee version of my childhood home, which was one of the reasons I loved it. Okay, so, good, we're building on a solid foundation.

Card Number Four (Recent Past)

Three of Cups

This card represents your recent past. For myself, I think of it as the past few months to the past few weeks. The Three of Cups is the "Hooray for Domesticity Card," happy in love, happy in life. Also indicates success in the arts, creative juices flowing. A room of one's own, and all that good stuff.

This card echoed the central card, which showed how happy I was working at home. That happiness had also led to some creative success, so, again, lots of happiness in the past and present. But, of course, I wondered why all these cards were showing up in the past and present. I wondered why, if my present living situation was so great, how come I was changing it?

Card Number Five (Best and Worst)

Four of Wands

Ah, now we're getting to the future! Here's where most of us really start paying attention. The card in this position is the near future, the not-as-strong future. What happens here either may or may not happen, or it may not be lasting.

The Four of Wands represents the rewards of your labor. A rich, overflowing home, filled with contentment and peace of mind. It's the first date with the guy you just know you're going to marry, it's the job interview that went perfectly, it's Christmas with the Peanuts Special. Again, it's a card I want to see as the Final Card. Not the maybe, near future card.

But I'll take it. Definitely.

Card Number Six (Future Influence)

Death, Reversed

Okay, here we are, looking at things that will happen in the future. Not might happen, *will* happen. Needless to say, I looked at this card and freaked.

Nobody, but *nobody*, likes to see Death in any of the future positions. Even I, with all my wisdom and knowledge about tarot, thought, "DEATH! I got DEATH in my reading! AGH! Call the broker right now, call the whole thing off!"

I started chanting my Death Card Mantra: "Death is not that bad. It just means change. The end of an old life, the beginning of a new. Blah, blah, blah. . . ."

Then I saw it was reversed and thought, I'm screwed.

So, what does Death Reversed in the sixth position mean? The sixth card reflects the future, but it's only an influence on the future, an aspect of it. It is not the *outcome*. It's a person, a new path. It has definite power. But it's not the be-all and end-all.

But it's true that Death Reversed is not as positive as Death Right Side Up. There's no happy ending, no new life with Death Reversed. Instead, it shows the inability to move on. To acknowledge change and embrace the new. You're sort of hanging on, whining, "It was so much better before."

It's also the downside of change. Change without purpose. Violence. Recklessness. The part in the French Revolution when they stop singing the "Marseillaise" and start chopping off heads.

So, this meant two things to me. I was going to miss Brooklyn. I wasn't going to have a smooth, easy transition where everything is better in the New World. Probably I would feel most depressed and whiny during the chaos and hell of actually moving, when you're neither here nor there, and everything you need is in boxes. But, because the card is in the sixth position, I told myself the feeling would not be permanent. It is not the *outcome*. (Thank God, Thank God, Thank God. . . .)

Card Number Seven (Self-Image)

The Devil

If I have to get the Devil right after Death, I want him here, as my Fears and Neuroses Card. Unlike Death, which has a lovely vision of rebirth, there's no positive way to spin the Devil. He represents addiction, total bondage to something that makes you miserable. Was I afraid of being in a strange place, bound by debt, wondering why I ever thought I could happy here? You bet.

But that's my fear, not my reality. However, this card shows my fears are pretty intense. What do you want from me? I'm neurotic.

Card Number Eight (Other People's Vision)

Eight of Swords

I call the card in this position the "cootie card." It shows the dynamic you have with other people, the ways your actions affect how they respond to you.

Swords generally indicate combat. With the Eight of Swords, you see someone who's too terrified to budge, even in the face of danger—in a complete state of dithering panic, deer in the headlights. Given Card Number Seven, this is obviously me.

Now, since I am *not* going to call the broker and call off the move, what's the impact of my fears on my situation and on those around me? The probable problem I can think of is that I would procrastinate. Put off packing. Not call the people I had to call. Dither around until I wind up doing everything at the last minute—or leave it for my husband to do. The result of that? Like I said, Swords indicate combat.

Note to self: be organized. Do not procrastinate. Don't let anxieties prevent you from moving forward.

Card Number Nine (Hopes and Fears)

Justice

If Card Number Seven shows me my fears, Card Number Nine shows me my hopes. Now, Justice isn't a particularly "homey" card. It offers balance between the public and the private. Your emotions and the situation. And yes, career and home, nicely stabilized. It suggests a new start, free of old prejudices. What I find interesting here is that my hopes, like my anxieties, largely center on how the home affects my writing career. Hopefully, I'll love writing in my new study. Hopefully childish ideas like "Queens just isn't as 'cool' as Brooklyn" won't stand in the way of enjoying everything my new neighborhood has to offer.

Okay, at last. Here it is . . . The Final Outcome!

Card Ten (The Final Outcome)

The Four of Swords

As I said, what I would love to see here is the Four of Wands or the Sun. But that's not what's here.

The Four of Swords is a very logical final card for this reading. Death Reversed showed that this move will not be entirely smooth. The Devil reveals part of the reason by showing the intense anxiety I have over the issue. And no move is ever trouble-free. Change is exhilarating—and it also sucks.

The Four of Swords shows peace and quiet—but not like a happy walk in the woods with birds singing. This isn't rest you enjoy, it's rest you *need*. It's the calm after the storm, taking a step back after tumultuous times. You're exhausted, your nerves are on edge, and you just want some time to yourself, goddamn it.

All very appropriate after moving.

It's also a card of transition. The words exile and abandonment characterize this card. So it tells me that I will *not* be leaping into a whirl of social activity, happy as a clam, and thinking, *Wow, I don't miss Brooklyn a bit.* There will be some funk and gloom and second thoughts. I wish it were otherwise, but given who I am and the size of the change, it's not logical to expect that. I'll need time to really feel at home. However, I can feel pretty certain that I will. Why? Because of cards one through five. They showed a really solid foundation for this move: an inner life and a relationship that can travel anywhere. They reminded me that a home isn't the four walls, but the life you create within those four walls. And the Four of Swords indicates a *temporary* rest. Once everything's unpacked, and a few weeks have gone by, I'll be feeling ready to explore and connect.

SAMPLE READING NUMBER TWO
THE NOVELIST

I sat down with a friend of mine who's a novelist. He is married with one child. He's had one novel published to great reviews, but first novels—even with great reviews—don't pull in a lot of money. Two years ago, he lost his job. At first, he saw it as a prime opportunity to really get down to work on his second novel. Then the inevitable need to eat and pay the rent struck and he took on a ton of freelance work. This had slowed down the novel's progress and, recently, he'd been feeling somewhat stuck. It wasn't writer's block, more like writer's blah. So his question to the cards was...

What is the future of my novel—creatively?

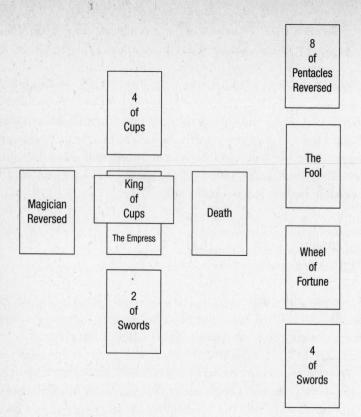

Card Number One (Present Position)

The Empress

The Empress represents fertility and creativity—which you would hope to see at the heart of a reading about a novel. It's a strong, healthy card, a card of inspiration and accomplishment. So we know the basic elements for novel writing are present.

Interestingly, the Empress also represents degrees of practicality and domestic matters—factors that would prove relevant as the reading went on.

Card Number Two (Immediate Influence)

The King of Cups

More creativity! The king of creativity! Here we have an artist, a sensitive soul, a generous spirit. The King of Cups isn't some flake who paints on the wall with his toes. A responsible person, he has the ability to profit from his talents.

So, at the core of this reading, we have two very powerful cards representing the creative drive. You even have a man and a woman who would make a lovely couple. But this also reminds us of the realities of the larger world. Neither of these figures operates in a vacuum. You can see the Empress as dominant in the home, while the King of Cups, the artist/businessman, is comfortable in the world of commerce.

Card Number Three (Distant Past)

The Two of Swords

In our Freudian Card, we have a vision of forces that match and balance each other. This is the *klang!* card, the moment when two strengths meet and neither side gives way. It represents either a perfect match or a stalemate—a clash that inspires or destroys.

My friend's mother had also been a novelist. But, throughout his childhood in the '50s and '60s, the demands on wives and mothers made it difficult for her to pursue a creative life as well. While she had received serious professional encouragement, my friend's mother didn't succeed as she might have liked to. So this card could represent a balance/tension between the creative life and the domestic life—which my friend experienced in his own life as well.

Card Number Four (Recent Past)

The Magician Reversed

Had this card been right side up, I would have said to my friend, "More creativity? Go home and write your novel. I can find no reason you're stuck."

However, the card was upside down, which was very interesting. Upside down, the Magician represents everything that stops us from doing what we know we should. It symbolizes procrastination, uncertainty, anxiety. It also corresponds to the use of your skills or talents for destructive (possibly self-destructive?) purposes.

This card confirmed that my friend was indeed having trouble writing his novel, and that the obstacles were, to a large degree, self-imposed. He had a mental, emotional block. So, what had caused the block? And would he get rid of it?

Card Number Five (Best and Worst)

The Four of Cups

The general gist of this card is disappointment. Disgust. Bitterness. It's a point in your life when everything seems so pointless, you can't go on. The best you can manage is to sit under a tree and be depressed.

This is your best and worst-case scenario card. Here, ideally, we would see more of that creative flow, with hints of cash and critical acclaim to follow. Why such a gloomy picture?

I couldn't really imagine my friend being disgusted with a project he loved, so I discarded the idea that he might have become fed up with the novel. I could, however, imagine that the pressures of making a living coupled with the will to create could become intolerable. That, at some point, he might say, "Screw it, I don't have the time for this, I'm going to stop pouring my energies into something that doesn't put food on the table." But I couldn't really imagine my friend being happy with that choice.

Or, he might try to continue as he has—trying to earn money

and put serious time and energy into his novel. But, to some degree, that's what got him stuck creatively in the first place. So I could also see that leading to a sense of frustration.

One interesting point with this card: the traditional image shows a young man sitting under a tree. He's staring at three cups with a look of contempt and boredom. Another cup is held out to him, but he pays no attention. There's a sense that he is being offered something that would bring him a lot of pleasure and happiness, but for some reason, he's choosing to ignore it.

This aspect of the card shows the escape route from disappointment and despair. If my friend can identify that, this card will serve as a warning only.

Card Number Six (Future Influence)

Death

When I asked my friend if he wanted me to do a reading, he said, "Fine, as long as I don't get that creepy skeleton card."

So, of course, he got the creepy skeleton card.

In the context of this reading, I felt 99 percent certain that this card did not predict physical death. To me, this card was good news. It means radical transformation, a change so profound it feels like the death of one life *in order to make way for the new one.* This is the end of a familiar situation. Money versus art has been a constant issue in my friend's life—as it is in the lives of most creative people. Since earlier cards had indicated conflicting obligations, and a state of depression and inertia that might result, I felt that a big shake-up was just what this situation called for. Something had to give way here. There would be loss involved; in change, there's always loss.

Would it be loss of the tension or loss of the creativity? Because the cards preceding Death represented the sense of frustration with his novel—as opposed to the creativity shown at the core of the reading—it seemed more likely that Death would resolve the tension rather than put an end to my friend's creative life.

Death also suggests financial loss and illness—two realities you can never overlook. But they're not the dominant themes, and since the dominant themes of creativity and cataclysmic change were so relevant in this reading, I chose to go with that.

Card Number Seven (Self-Image)

Four of Swords

Interestingly, one thing I say about the Four of Swords is that it is not a Death card, even though its image is somewhat funereal. Considering the Death card that just came up, clearly the end of something is much on my friend's mind.

This card can embody two slightly conflicting meanings. One is a proper rest, a time of peace and recharging after strenuous effort. The other is plain old quitting, abandonment, and loss. This reflects my friend's anxiety over the creative lull with his novel. Is it a productive time of stepping back, assessing, and letting the subconscious mind come up with brilliance? Or is he just procrastinating and stuck?

Card Number Eight (Other People's Vision)

The Wheel of Fortune

At first, I could *not* figure out this card. How could fate and destiny and big things coming to pass be related to other people's opinion of my friend and his novel?

The only way it made sense is that other people might feel strongly affected by my friend's commitment to his writing, that the completion/success of his novel mattered, not only to him, but to those around him. Given the tensions between the drive to write and the need to earn money, this card hinted that his novel might be carrying a heavier burden than creative endeavors can usually stand.

Card Number Nine (Hopes and Fears)

The Fool

Ask my friend, ask any writer, what they really want, and they will tell you they want to write and not give a good goddamn about life's practicalities. The Fool is an image of frightening optimism. You're stepping out into the world with nothing but high hopes and your talent. The fact that you may take your first step right off a cliff is of no consequence. In fact, the riskiness of the journey makes it interesting. This card reflects a very understandable wish on my friend's part to write in peace—and perhaps a less understandable infatuation with the grand, the impossible, and the impractical.

Card Number Ten (The Final Outcome)

The Eight of Pentacles Reversed

Pentacles is the money suit. The Eight of Pentacles Right Side Up represents the young go-getter who's eager to learn and willing to do any amount of shitwork to get ahead. He's an excellent employee—dedicated to craftsmanship, and modest, to boot.

Turn him upside down however and we have a different story. Here our young apprentice is a bitter burnt out case. He takes two-hour lunches and spends his afternoon goofing off on the web. He feels he's going nowhere, no one appreciates his talent, so what does it matter if he works hard or not?

This is not the final card I wanted to see for my friend. I wasn't sure if it depicted his feelings about the corporate world he was considering reentering or his feelings about a publishing climate hostile toward literary fiction. Significantly, it showed someone who allowed disappointment to cripple his pleasure in his work for its own sake—to the extent that he internalized the world's apparent indifference and said, No one cares about this, why the hell should I?

In short, this reading was an immensely strong core of talent and creativity, surrounded by stresses, obligations, and the occasional whiff of despair. The goal, here, it seemed to me, was to free our Empress and King of Cups from all the garbage surrounding them. In practical terms, I decided my friend needed to completely separate the novel from all other considerations in his life, both mentally and physically, by finding a set time that belonged to the novel and only to the novel. That time could not be impinged upon by family, freelance, or anything else. During that hour or two, he can be the Fool, striding confidently into the creative unknown without regard for financial or family consequences.

SAMPLE READING NUMBER THREE
SHE WHO GETS DUMPED LAUGHS LAST

I met with a young woman whose boyfriend of eight years had suddenly broken up with her. She had not seen it coming at all, and his reasons—as relayed by her—sounded vague and unspecific. She had the strong feeling that his family had exerted some pressure. She seemed sharp, intelligent, and perceptive, not the type to lie to herself any longer than any of us do during a breakup. But she confessed she was in the "wishful thinking" stage, and so she wanted to ask the cards . . .

Will we get back together and will we be happy?

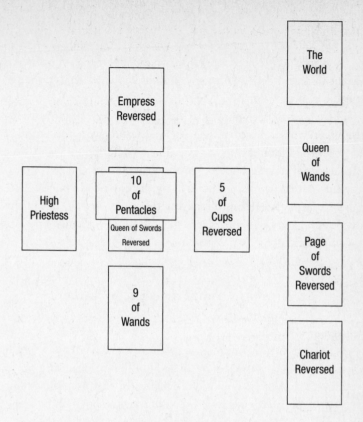

Card Number One (Present Position)

The Queen of Swords Reversed

The Queen of Swords Right Side Up is very much a card I would have expected to see at the heart of a reading about a breakup. She symbolizes loss, abandonment, a woman experiencing a reversal of fortune. But here she was upside down. What did that mean?

When this queen is upside down, you know exactly why no one wants to be around her. She's a narrow-minded bigot. She sees what she wants to, and usually it's a negative vision. She's carping, deceitful, and a dangerous enemy.

In no way could I reconcile this level of malice with the woman sitting opposite me. She hadn't spoken bitterly about the boyfriend or even his family. The element of deceit and negativity in the card made me wonder if perhaps she was blaming the family as a way to not lay blame on the boyfriend with whom she hoped to reconnect. Was she insisting they had a narrow view of her when, in fact, she had a narrow view of them?

There was another possibility here: The Queen of Swords Reversed represented the atmosphere she was dealing with, the nature of her current situation. From the questioner's description, it did seem genuinely as if she were subject to unfair judgment and self-serving criticism—either by the boyfriend or by the boyfriend's family. Usually, the center card relates directly to the reader herself, but in this case, I found it more likely that it was related to her situation. This woman just did not radiate shrew in any way.

Card Number Two (Immediate Influence)

The Ten of Pentacles

When I saw this card, I immediately asked if the boyfriend's family had money. She said yes, they did. The Ten of Pentacles is the Kennedy card: wealth, family, inheritance. In this position, it suggested that the questioner was right and that the boyfriend's family was playing a role here—or at least his sense of his obligations to the family was.

Card Number Three (Distant Past)

Nine of Wands

In this woman's "Freudian" card, I found an image of strength and preparedness. It does have some anticipation of battle, but no one's rushing out to bash someone on the head. They're just ready to deal with whatever comes. Not knowing anything about her childhood or her parents' marriage, I took this as a sign that the questioner was a calm and stable person, not prone to overreaction or dramatics. The card suggested someone who fared well in a crisis—something that would prove significant later on in the reading.

Card Number Four (Recent Past)

The High Priestess

Ah, the platonic card. The High Priestess is something of a scholar reclusive and serene. She embodies common sense and self-reliance. She's not, admittedly, a lot of fun—who wants to be so grown up and in control all the time? But, in the position of the recent past, she indicates that while the questioner has certainly been spending more time on her own lately, she's using that time well. Nobody's boiling rabbits or making weird phone calls at two in the morning. She might hope that the breakup is temporary—but she's doing just fine without him. It's exactly what I would expect from someone with the well of strength and calm depicted in Card Number Three.

Card Number Five (Best and Worst)

The Empress Reversed

Again, it's always interesting when the cards decide to flop upside down. The Empress Right Side Up would have meant happiness, marriage, fruitfulness—the epitome of traditional feminine happiness and a good sign that the breakup would be, or should be, temporary.

But upside down, it represents another scenario familiar to most women: half-assed commitment. Uncertainty. Indecision. Refusal to commit, refusal to let go. A sort of lover's limbo. You can easily interpret this to mean a reconciliation gone wrong. Everyone's back, but nothing feels quite right. The questioner had said specifically that she wished to be happy. This didn't show a vision of joy and security. I saw it as a warning that if the boyfriend did decide to reconcile, she should stick to her guns about the quality of relationship she wanted. Or, if he remained out of the picture, she shouldn't let herself go on wishing for too long, but rather open herself up to new opportunities (always easier said than done). In short, she should remember her inner High Priestess and not settle for less than she deserves.

Card Number Six (Future Influence)

The Five of Cups Reversed

Well, well, remember those new opportunities we said our questioner might be looking for? Here they are. This is a very happy card to see in your near future position. It's connotes getting past disappointment and moving on. It's good omens, favorable winds, the universe smiling upon you. Rather maddeningly for this questioner, it can mean either a new alliance (i.e., man on the horizon) or the return of a loved one. Either way, what's crucial here is the chance to escape the quagmire of indecision and unhappiness depicted in Card Number Five.

Card Number Seven (Self-Image)

The Chariot Reversed

The Chariot itself shows us a woman speeding down the highway of life, confident, self-assured, maybe a little reckless—but with such style, who cares? The Chariot Reversed shows us the same woman, only the car's hit a serious skid and she's badly shaken up.

This card denotes a sudden reversal of fortune. You think everything's fine—as did our reader with her relationship—then, all of a sudden, wham! It entails sudden collapse, possibly the result of a failure to confront reality. People you thought were your friends, lovers, allies, have turned on you. You're self-doubting, overwhelmed, and feeling not too steady on your feet. In short, how you'd feel after a breakup.

However, I reminded the questioner of the High Priestess. She may see herself as the shell-shocked victim of a car wreck, but that's not how she's conducted herself at all. Her head is on straight, no matter how whiplashed she feels.

Card Number Eight (Other People's Vision)

The Page of Swords Reversed

Remember our stout, hardy youth from Card Number Three? The lad prepared for anything? This is his much weaker, befuddled brother. Pleasant enough, but he gets shouted down in every family argument. He's easily defeated by those stronger than he, shoved aside—partly because he didn't see the shove coming. This card also hints of pretense, as if he promised everyone he could handle it, then fell asleep and didn't have a clue when the fighting started.

Since this position shows us Other People's Vision of our questioner, it's crucial to figure out whose vision we're talking about. First thing that came to mind was the questioner's friends. Perhaps they felt she should be taking a stronger position with her boyfriend, challenging him on his decision to put his family above her. Perhaps they had seen it coming, and she hadn't, and they were privately tut-tutting over her "lack of preparedness."

But that interpretation didn't feel very satisfying to me, as it didn't square with cards Three or Four. Plus, friends seemed kind of beside the point. What seemed more likely was that this was the view of the boyfriend himself. The crucial element—weak in the face of a strong opponent—reflected the choice she sensed he had made in placing his parents' demands ahead of their relationship. What was most interesting was how little this had to do with her as an individual. Unless her boyfriend had privately felt she needed to be "stronger" somehow, he seems to have made his decision on the Squeaky Wheel premise. The parents screamed loudest; he gave them what they wanted—whatever that was.

Card Number Nine (Hopes and Fears)

The Queen of Wands

The Queen of Wands is just the best person. She's warm, nonjudgmental, and has an earthy sense of humor. Completely secure within herself and her domain, she never feels the need to be bitchy or undermining. As a wife, she's loving, honorable, and will never do her man dirty.

For a Hope and Fears card, this is an extremely healthy vision. (Let's face it, most of us hope for big love, big money, or fame.) This seemed to be an image of selfhood that the reader wanted, a level of security and generosity that would be pretty irresistible to anyone in a marrying frame of mind—*but that didn't insist on marriage*. While the Queen of Wands is exactly who you want your best friend or brother to end up with, she's not strictly about marriage. (Check out the Queen of Cups if you want the hausfrau.) She's content within herself and all her other relationships. This, I thought, showed an excellent distinction between being happy and being with someone. It supported what the questioner had said: that she only wanted to resume the relationship if she and he would be happy together.

Card Number Ten (Final Outcome)

The World

When this card turned up, I told the questioner, "Well, it's a happy ending."

It's very, very rare that the World turns up as your Final Outcome. It represents happiness, perfection, fulfillment of all hopes and dreams, triumph after a hard struggle. You've put in the effort and now you reap the rewards. It's the Snoopy Happy Dance of cards. Readings seldom end with such a positive or definitive conclusion.

So, what did this mean? Would the boyfriend come back, chastened but wiser? Would the separation prove beneficial to their relationship? If resumption of the relationship was truly what the reader was hoping for, then this card would strongly suggest a rapturous return and a new and improved level of their relationship.

And we can leave it at that. Except that the Hopes and Fears card did not show us a boyfriend or marriage. In fact, nowhere in the entire reading, except for Card Number Eight, did I see the boyfriend at all. This could reflect his state of total absence right now. But this reading was most positive when it was about the questioner herself. With or without the boyfriend, she was on track (according to the

High Priestess and the Five of Cups Reversed) to break into a new, exciting stage of her life. The Empress Reversed suggested that she faced a danger of remaining anxious and indecisive about moving on—particularly in the realm of love. I am biased against dumpers, I admit this. So, I'm tempted to read this as a vision of the questioner taking this unexpected change in her life as an opportunity to chart a new and very promising path for herself. Then, if he comes back, she can take him back if she wants to and on her terms.

SAMPLE READING NUMBER FOUR
LOOKING FOR LOVE FOR ALL THE WRONG REASONS?

I did a reading for an old friend of mine. Like a lot of us, she was trying to find her footing in various aspects of life, from romance to career. An immensely bright and talented person, she's aware that she hasn't gone nearly as far with her gifts as she'd like to, and was struggling to rid herself of things that might be holding her back.

Her question to the cards was...

When will I meet someone who will support me enough to achieve the things I want to achieve?

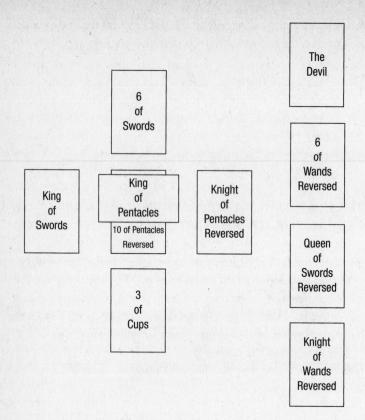

Card Number One (Present Position)

The Ten of Pentacles, Reversed

One image you might choose for the Ten of Pentacles Reversed is the Gambler. It seems like fun in the beginning, a little carefree bet here and there, low risk with the potential for big gains. Then, all of a sudden, you're in the hole, and you're frantically raising the stakes trying to win it all back with one hand . . . and still losing.

Dissipated efforts, loss of resources, time and energy, a growing sense of anxiety. That was my friend's state of mind right now. In the past, she had held several jobs, but she had never found one that felt like a life's calling. At the same time, she hadn't had the time to fully commit to the things she really loved, such as cooking and performing. Now she had both the resolve and the pressure to find her path.

Card Number Two (Immediate Influence)

The King of Pentacles
The King of Pentacles is a powerful, responsible guy with big bucks and a good heart. You could see him as Daddy Warbucks. He seemed to fit the bill for my friend's vision of someone who would support her (although I had thought she meant emotionally rather than financially, but perhaps the two were blending a bit?).

My friend was dating, but her current beau was not equipped to take on this role. She was living at home, which meant that her mom and dad provided some support. Her dad was a businessman. So was he our King of Pentacles?

It seemed most likely to me that rather than an actual guy on the horizon, this king represented my friend's vision of the solution to her dilemma: a strong, mature man who loved her and made her feel special enough to face the world on her own terms.

Card Number Three (The Distant Past)

The Three of Cups
This is a very happy card, a vision of people coming together to resolve their problems and, then celebrating the peace with a big party. I don't know how my friend saw this, but I immediately thought of her family. Like any family, they have their issues, but they are funny, generous, cultured people who invite you over, put great food on the table, and make you feel at home. The parents are deeply involved in their daughters' lives.

My friend might disagree, but whatever the actual group represented here, it was clear she was drawing on a memory of support and safety and happiness that involved other people. This can be a positive, as it's good to have such a great example of human interaction. It can be a negative if it means going it alone scares you.

Card Number Four (Recent Events)

The King of Swords

So many kings in this reading! Lots of powerful men. The King of Swords is the most commanding of them all. He represents judgment, a reality check, a short, sharp shock to the system. He's the doctor who tells you you need to quit drinking or your liver will explode. He's the bank guy who tells you your credit's cut off. He can also be the boss who gives you a big fat promotion. Not because he's a nice guy and he likes you, but because it's the fair and just thing to do.

This situation called for objective assessment, and that's what we had here—the sword that cuts through denial. Recently, my friend had had a few experiences that brought her up short, prompting her to take stock of where she was and where she wanted to go. One of them involved a cop. My friend had not been arrested, but for several reasons, he seemed like a good candidate for the King of Swords to me.

Card Number Five (Best and Worst)

The Six of Swords

The happiest words here are "success after anxiety." Yay! This card depicts a real attempt to overcome past difficulties, a journey into the unknown. It hints at haste, a sense of "Screw it, let's get it over with!" This, my friend should watch. But the overall results are usually positive.

This is the best my friend can achieve in her current state of mind. It's a lot. It shows a real attempt to make positive changes and move forward. Please note: no kings or knights or Prince Charmings here. Her own effort, her own work, would garner this success. If the King of Swords represented a man who had come into her life recently, then he might be the agent of this change. But as no one new had come into her life lately, I discounted this.

Card Number Six (Future Influence)

The Knight of Pentacles Reversed

Yuck. Not a card you want to see when you're trying to change your life. This connotes inertia, procrastination, screw it, I'll do it tomorrow. It symbolizes falling prey to old, bad habits and preconceptions. We are all so familiar with this feeling—and we all know how it holds us back. Yet, we reach for the remote and the Cheetos and decide that we'll deal with it . . . whenever.

This card meant that in the future, my friend was going to face a very strong challenge in her attempt to achieve a breakthrough. It could be a mood, an event, a person—anything that distracts, depresses, and demoralizes her. When it came, she would have to recognize it and fight, fight, fight. Hide that remote! Throw away the Cheetos!

I suggested that now would probably be a good time to make a list of to-dos that would help her in her goals. Contact five potential clients, clean closet . . . whatever would keep her focused on her own future during this time of aggravation.

Card Number Seven (Self-Image)

The Knight of Wands Reversed

The Knight of Wands Right Side Up represents that great headlong leap into the unknown. He's Moving Day, a journey both physical and psychic.

Upside down, he depicts the restlessness and irritability that might precede such a move—or might occur if the move should have happened, but didn't. It indicates a sense of rupture, dissatisfaction with existing relationships, breakdown of old ties. Those you relied on in the past are not coming through as they used to—or maybe you just need different things at this point in time. It can also represent unexpected change.

This card indicated that my friend's primary sense of herself was of a person in flux, at odds with people she cared for, beset by events and emotions she didn't fully trust or feel in control of.

Card Number Eight (Other People's Vision)

The Queen of Swords Reversed

The Queen of Swords Reversed is a nasty, narrow-minded old bag. Treacherous, malicious, she sees everything through the grimy lens of her own disappointments and shortcomings.

Now, my friend is human and so has flaws, but none of these fit the bill to my mind. And frankly, I couldn't imagine in whose mind they would fit the bill. If anything, she has a tendency to be too up and optimistic. It seemed an odd card for her to get, even in the often bewildering position of Other People's Vision.

The one word that fit at all was judgmental. My friend admitted she has a tendency to judge people, at times harshly. I encouraged her to think about a key relationship where that habit might be a problem, and we left it at that.

Card Number Nine (Hopes and Fears)

Six of Wands Reversed

"The only thing we have to fear is fear itself." FDR said it and, apparently, my friend agrees. The Six of Wands Reversed represents fear, anxiety, delay with no movement in sight, advancement so small that it's all but meaningless.

This is a very self-aware Hopes and Fears card. My friend has put her finger on exactly what's holding her back: her own anxieties. She's most afraid that she won't be able to get rid of them, and they'll continue to dictate her progress—or lack of it. Of course, it's very easy to say: Don't be afraid! There's no monster in that closet! It's quite another thing to actually banish the fear. Or—what's more likely—do what you have to, no matter how scared you are.

Card Number Ten (The Final Outcome)

The Devil

When someone gets the Devil at the end of their reading, you have to take a deep breath and stay calm. It's a very serious card. To my mind, it's worse than Death. The Devil has no redeeming traits. He's helplessness, addiction, masochism . . . the bonds that not only hold us back, but destroy us. If the Devil held true, my friend was not going to be able to realize any of her goals. Not only would her situation not improve, it would most likely grow worse.

However, there was an up side: this could well be a Devil she already knew. To my way of thinking, my friend had defined the Devil in the way she asked the question: *When will I meet someone who will support me enough to achieve the things I want to?* We all need support. We all need love. But relying on someone else to make you feel strong enough to go in search of the life you want . . . you might as well invite Beelzebub to dinner and hold your hands out while he snaps on the chains. That's how much power you're giving away to someone you haven't even met yet. To me, this meant my friend should be reassessing every aspect of dependency in her life, and working to make herself a free and independent woman. Forget the King of Pentacles! Forget Daddy Warbucks and Prince Charming—storm the castle now!

Now, other things might come to my friend's mind when she thinks of the Devil: relationships, self-destructive habits, old patterns. And the Devil can represent some unexpected evil coming at you like a thunderbolt. But in most cases, you make the deal with the Devil. You go along with it somehow. Which means you can make the choice not to—however hard that might be.

The Six of Swords held out the promise that my friend had it within her to make the changes she wanted. However, the rest of the reading presented nothing but obstacles—most of which I also felt were within her to some degree. We agreed to do another reading in a month.

SAMPLE READING NUMBER FIVE
FEAR AND LOATHING IN LOVE'S DOMAIN

This questioner was in her mid-thirties, attractive, intelligent, and engaged in an interesting line of work. At this point in her life, issues of marriage and children began to crop up. She was dating, but finding it hard to meet someone she found appealing enough for the goals she had in mind.

She chose not to tell me her question until after the reading. Had she told me beforehand, I would have urged her to narrow the scope a little. But the cards yielded fascinating results, nonetheless.

Her question was...

When am I going to meet someone and have the life I think I want?

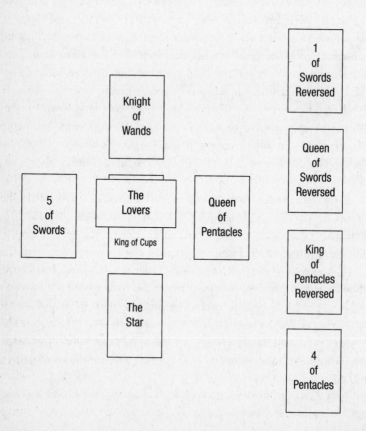

Card Number One (Present Position)

The King of Cups

The King of Cups in the Present position of a reading about relationships strongly implies a love interest. The questioner is asking about someone in particular whom they have just met or with whom they're in a relationship.

Most women, if they met the King of Cups, would like to date him. He's both creative and responsible, scholarly but not stuffy. He could be a lawyer or a playwright. If a lawyer, he has a keen interest in the arts; if a playwright, he's either successful or has a nice big trust fund. He's a king, which means he's a grown-up, not some dippy kid. Sounds like marriage material to me.

Card Number Two (Immediate Influence)

The Lovers

If I had any doubt that this was a question about relationships, this card obliterated it. The questioner was ready to be in love. Now, several cards represent love and family matters. The Lovers is possibly the most idealistic and/or naive out of all of them. It can represent a healthy level of optimism and trust. It can also represent those early, heady days when you have nothing but illusions about each other. Or a vision of love through the Hollywood lens—no long, boring relationship discussions, no compromises, just passion and infatuation and perfection.

The two cards together represented some interesting crossroads and conflicts. The King of Cups, as I said, is ideal marriage material. Cups is the suit of the heart, with the king its most powerful representative. He told me the questioner was not looking for just a good "catch"—as might be represented by the King of Pentacles for example. She wanted a well-rounded man capable of having a fun, nurturing relationship with her.

The Lovers suggested that she was feeling emotionally ambitious, ready to take some risks—provided she found a man worth taking them for. There was a romantic, idealistic streak here. The questioner struck me as a sensible, even somewhat cautious person. But this card seemed to suggest that she felt that if she was going to put herself out there romantically, she wanted the Real Thing. Not just settling for Mr. Okay. She wanted a touch of the whirlwind, to be swept off her feet a bit, thank you very much.

Ideal man. True love. The lady was shooting high.

Card Number Three (Distant Past)

The Star

The Star is one of the most confusing and contradictory cards in the whole tarot deck. It can mean hope and bright prospects as well as loss and abandonment. As the "Freudian" card of a relationship reading, it should depict the questioner's early experiences with love and marriage—either the example of her parents' relationship or a significant romance in her own past. I didn't want to pry, so I didn't ask the questioner how she herself read this card. But among the possible scenarios that might fit were . . . 1) an excellent example of marriage that shaped the questioner's high expectations, or 2) the loss of such a relationship.

Card Number Four (Recent Past)

The Five of Swords

Well, here was a card that indicated that the questioner's recent forays into *l'amour* had not been happy ones. Swords generally have no place in a reading about love, and this card evokes such loaded words as degradation, defeat, and dishonor. Great. Not at all the kind of thing you hope for when looking for true love—but, sadly, the kind of thing many of us find.

Card Number Five (Best and Worst)

The Knight of Wands

This was much better news. Traditionally, the court cards represent people of some kind. The Knight of Wands can represent a dark-haired young man, if you want to be all literal about it.

The Knight of Wands can also predict a journey, advancement of some kind, a leap into the unknown. This definitely echoes the Lovers. It suggests that the questioner has it within herself to overcome the disappointments depicted by the Five of Swords and possibly the Star. Imagine a young man on horseback making a tremendous leap across a chasm. Will he land safely on the other side? We don't know—but that's part of the drama and excitement, isn't it?

Sometimes, the Best and Worst card warns of what you have to watch out for. Sometimes it's an example of what you can aspire to. Since we don't know the outcome here—safe landing or splat—we can't say for sure which the Knight of Wands represents. However, since the questioner seems interested in taking emotional risks, and since any foray into romance is risky, I would say overall that this was a positive card.

Card Number Six (Future Influence)

The Queen of Pentacles

If someone was looking to make a great leap forward, the Queen of Pentacles is an excellent guiding spirit. She represents liberty that derives from a strong sense of security. She has so much, she shares freely with others. A strong sense of self gives her a wonderful air of confidence and graciousness.

I had a sense that this questioner did not take emotional risks lightly. It seemed important to her not to make self-destructive choices, even to the point where she might second-guess some things she ought to take on faith. So, the Queen of Pentacles was good news for her. It indicated that in the near future, for whatever reason—personal insight, a promotion at her job, a fabulous new haircut—the questioner would be feeling powerful enough to make new connections, secure in the knowledge that should she hook up with a dragon rather than Prince Charming, she was tough enough to handle him.

Card Number Seven (Self-Image)

The Four of Pentacles

The Queen of Pentacles spreads the wealth; the Four of Pentacles is a tightwad. Money is way too important to this person. They hoard it, hug it. They share with no one. The word "miser" is not inappropriate here.

This is a harsh card to get for your Self-Image. Generally, the suit of Pentacles represents money, but here I think we can stretch it to an overall sense of generosity—both emotional and materialistic. This is an image of a woman afraid to give for fear people will take advantage of her. Offer a little, and someone's just going to take and take and take. She's well aware that keeping all her wealth to herself doesn't really make her happy, but at least she doesn't feel like a fool.

That this card turns up as the Self-Image suggests the questioner's anxiety about her ability to open up to people. She wants to take the leap of faith, to give herself over to the vision of high romance depicted by the Lovers—but she's worried she won't be able to. That fear may well founded, it may not. Let's see what other people have to say. . . .

Card Number Eight (Other People's Vision)

The King of Pentacles Reversed

Okay, the upside here is that the questioner can gain self-awareness. Her fear that she comes off as somewhat emotionally stingy is not totally unfounded. The King of Pentacles Reversed has a ruthless, ungiving character. He's a taker who puts himself first—and he plays dirty. He's about money, status, and his own skin.

As always with Other People's Vision, we have to bear in mind whose vision we're seeing. Are they reliable? Or, are they biased to the point of irrelevance? The questioner will have to figure out who might see her this way, and then decide how seriously to take this opinion. If the person in question is an ex whom she's well rid of, then it doesn't matter. If it's someone she misses or is hoping to attract, then she wants to rethink her approach.

Card Number Nine (Hopes and Fears)

Queen of Swords Reversed

If you asked me to describe the mother-in-law from hell, she'd end up sounding a lot like the Queen of Swords Reversed. She is a nasty piece of work, bigoted, foul-tempered, and malicious. Oh, and she's a big fat prude.

So, why is she turning up as the questioner's Hopes and Fears card? Is she a romantic rival? A potential mother-in-law? Her own mom? Given the fact that this queen echoes some of the traits found in the cards in positions six and seven, it seems far more likely to me that she reflects the questioner's fears about herself and her future. *No one* would want to be with this woman except a confirmed masochist. Also, earlier, the questioner had spoken feelingly about dishonesty and disconnect in relationships; this card could represent a vision of marital deceit. Everyone puts on a big smile when the guests are around, but they're sticking knives in each other under the dinner table.

However, this is a *fear*, not a reality. It only influences the questioner's decisions; it doesn't determine her fate—unless she lets it.

Card Number Ten (The Final Outcome)

One of Swords Reversed

As the Final Outcome for this question, the One of Swords would have been ideal. It represents deep emotional commitment, triumph, fertility . . . just overall success to the point of excess.

Unfortunately, it's upside down, which indicates sort of the opposite: self-destruction instead of conquest, anger instead of passion, embarrassment as opposed to openness. It's a severe card with a lot of pain and upset.

All of which leads us to ask . . . why? The core desire of love and happiness, while perhaps ambitious in its purity, is not unhealthy in any way. There are hints of disappointment in the past, but only the past. The future suggests a journey into the unknown of some kind made with confidence and emotional openness. What the hell goes wrong?

Two out of the four most negative cards concern the questioner's fears and anxieties about herself. The person depicted in Other People's Vision will have an easy time in a romantic relationship. This suggests that she may be in a situation of self-fulfilling prophecy. The questioner might be aware that she holds back, yet privately believes that the minute she opens up, the Universe is going to say "Ha, ha!" and punish her for it. If this has already happened to her—and let's face it, it's happened to most of us—the fear could be pretty intense.

So, does she take the leap and disaster results? It's not nice to think so. Since we are talking about relationships here, it's hard to predict without knowing the other half of the sketch.

But I think the major clue lies in the contradiction between the intense idealism and romanticism at the core of the reading and the serious self-scrutiny and tendency to judge indicated in other parts of the reading. Expectations are both high and low: "I want and believe in true love" and "But it'll never happen for me, I always fall for jerks." There's not a lot of middle ground or room for error here. In that kind of scenario, a small setback can feel like the disaster depicted by the One of Swords Reversed. The key to avoiding that disaster, it would seem to me, would be for the questioner to examine her notion of true love—can it be a little less exalted?—and ease up on herself big time. The chasm she's trying to leap over is the gap between her vision of what constitutes a successful relationship and her nagging suspicion that it just isn't possible—at least for her.

Strange but True
Tales of Tarot Number Four

The Boy Who Broke Up Too Soon

*N**ow here's a prime example of how the person interpreting the tarot* can screw up a perfectly good reading. In this case, the interpreter was yours truly, and the questioner was a young man who had just taken a job with the company I worked for.

He had just moved to New York. But he had left something behind in his old town: a girlfriend. Right before he moved, he broke up with her. Why? Well, they had been going out since college. She wanted to get married and stay where they were; he didn't, and so they broke up.

At the time, he felt ready to move on, eager to take part in the great singles life in the city.

But he had one small problem: he really missed his ex-girlfriend.

And what he wanted to know from the cards was this: Had he done the right thing in breaking up with her, or was she the woman he was destined to be with?

Here's where my prejudices came into play. I don't believe in marrying your college sweetheart. After leaving school, too many couples just cling together, afraid to move on, afraid to take risks. Then, ten years into the marriage, they hate each other and neither one has a clue what went wrong.

So, privately, as he shuffles, I'm thinking: This is just breakup jitters. I'm sure the cards will tell him he made the right decision. There will be pain and disruption in the past and present. But happiness, new romance, and opportunities in the future.

Only that's not how the cards turned out.

Pain and disruption did appear in the recent past, all right. But the future cards held remorse. A sense of loss. Emptiness.

Still, I seized on the Eight of Cups, saying this indicated that he felt bad for no reason—looking to what he didn't have, when he should appreciate all the new opportunities he did have.

Now, you could also interpret this as someone who saw the glass as half-empty rather than half-full, and threw away a perfectly good beverage because of it.

But I didn't want this young man thinking he'd made a mistake. So I reassured him that the cards said he had done the right thing in breaking up with his girlfriend, that he was just experiencing a natural sense of dislocation, and that he should *move on*.

Bad, bad me.

My friend did move on. He dated a few other women, but he quickly discovered that the New York singles life ain't any more fun for guys than it is for women. After a few years, he got tired of our company and moved back home to take a terrific new job.

Oh, yeah, and he looked up his old girlfriend.

They were nice enough to invite me to the wedding.

How to Throw a Tarot Party

*T*ired *of movie night? Weary of shouting out your personal business in* a bar? Want to shake up the girls' night out routine?

Throw a tarot party.

Tarot parties are a really fun way to hang out with friends and discuss all that good personal stuff without getting too deep. A group of three to five is optimal; that way everyone gets a chance to really dig in. And, of course, you must tell the group what your question is. Otherwise, it's no fun. You can choose one person to do all the readings or rotate as each person does her own.

Some basic tarot party guidelines . . .

1. Decide ahead of time whether or not the peanut gallery can comment or if only the reader can interpret the cards.
2. If they are welcome, don't use the cards to make a point you've decided "needs" making. For example, don't say, "You've got the Two of Swords Reversed. That proves your boyfriend's cheating on you. In fact, I know he's cheating on you because I'm the one he's cheating with!"

3. Don't get too trashed when doing tarot. The readings get sloppy.

Good movies to rent for a tarot party:

1. *The Craft*
2. *The Witches of Eastwick*
3. *Practical Magic*

If you don't want to go with movies as a backdrop, music is good, too. Anything with a nice gothic overtone will do, from "Tubular Bells" to Kate Bush.

The Twenty-First Century Equivalent of "What's Your Sign?"

Here's another great use for tarot: meeting people. If you get invited to one of those parties where you don't know anyone, and you get the chance to do a reading for someone, do it. I guarantee you will be the most popular person at the party. Your only headache will be choosing a moment to leave because there will always be one more person who wants a reading.

N.B.: This does not work so well with meeting guys. Most guys think tarot is a "girly" thing, and will not be caught dead having a reading done, particularly in public. It is a great conversation starter, and a good way to find out things about a potential date, but proceed with caution.

. . . And Just For Yourself

*B*ut the best thing about tarot is that whenever you feel anxious or excited about the future, you can plop yourself down on the floor, or your bed, or your couch and take a peek into what lies ahead. A lot of people will tell you you can't do readings for yourself. I actually think you are the best qualified person to do your readings. Often tarot picks up on strange, subconscious stuff that it is very hard for the outside reader to define. Tarot gives you a snapshot, an x-ray of where and who you are at this given moment—and where you're likely to go if you proceed on your current path.

And, if you don't like where you're going, you have the power to change things. But that usually requires a level of insight and candor that very few outside tarot readers who are not your friends will be able to manage.

Is tarot foolproof? Nothing is foolproof. Not your mother's warnings, not your best friend's encouragement, not even your shrink.

But as I said way back when . . .

It's cheaper than Zoloft and less fattening than chocolate.